SCARS OF
SILENCE

An Amazing Journey of Survival

Mary Ann Worsham

SCARS OF SILENCE: AN AMAZING JOURNEY OF SURVIVAL
PUBLISHED BY BRIDGEWAY BOOKS
2100 KRAMER LANE, SUITE 300
AUSTIN, TEXAS 78758

For more information about our books, please write to us, call 512.478.2028, or visit our website at www.bookpros.com.

Newspaper articles and photographs reprinted with permission.

This book contains graphic content from real-life events.

Library of Congress Control Number: 2006930056

ISBN-10: 1-933538-62-7
ISBN-13: 978-1-933538-62-4

This book is dedicated to the true Author and Finisher of my story.
My Best Friend and Savior, Jesus Christ.

Contents

Chapter 1 1

Chapter 2 7

Chapter 3 23

Chapter 4 31

Chapter 5 39

Chapter 6 50

Chapter 7 71

Chapter 8 92

Chapter 9 96

Epilogue 106

Contact Resource List 112

Controlling People. 112

How to Not be Stressed Out,
Anxious and Fearful 115

How to Have Faith and Hope and
Battle Depression. 116

How to Forgive Others 123

Abortion / Adoption 130

Miscarriage / Loss of a Child. 134

Characteristics of a Crisis 136

Natural Disasters. .138

Eating Disorders 139

Setting Goals. 140

Information About Fraud 141

Sexual Harassment / Hostile
Work Environment 142

Problem Solving when Employment has
been Terminated: Identifying the issues 143

Domestic Violence and
Child Abuse / Neglect 144

American Legal System 149

Alcohol and Drug Abuse. 151

Forgiveness 154

Depression. 154

Your Responsibility to America. 155

Post-Traumatic Stress Disorder 156

Surgery 159

Head Injury. 166

Step / Blended Families 171

Aging Parents 173

Funeral History and Planning 175

Foreword

I am so happy to have the opportunity for you to read this and I count it as another blessing along my journey on the road of life. A lot of people would buy books by Nicole Brown Simpson, Chandra Levy, Laci Peterson or Mark Hacking's wife, because they want to know the "inside" story behind what they have heard on the news. The trouble is, people can't buy those books because those women can't tell their stories.

But I can. I am able to speak for them.

You see, I have literally been in their places, right up to the moment of death. But God has kept me here to continue to help others. I was asleep when I was attacked with a hammer, given twenty skull fractures, stabbed ten times, and left for dead. But I didn't die. Because of this important difference between me and the other women I have named, I can tell my story and, through it, shed light on theirs.

Since 1995, I have not been allowed — by law and for other reasons — to speak about what I have been through. Until now. And so now I will speak. My main desire is to help others and save lives — maybe even yours.

This book gives you the tools you will need to learn about and plan for a variety of events, from the most common everyday events to even the most difficult. There is no guarantee that life will work out the way we want it to. And so it is when people hurt us or when circumstances go out of control that we need to put into action some basic guidelines that will keep us going and get us to where we need to be. This book is filled with hands-on, useful information, including many ways to get free material and to contact people who can help you with your situation.

As you read this book, you will learn ways to look at adversity and use it to benefit yourself and the ones you love. It will also help you face some subjects that we sometimes avoid because they make us feel uncomfortable. One such subject is death. But remember, none of us will get out of this journey alive. With this book, you will be able to plan for what will happen before that time comes. You can consider helping others by giving them the gift of life and you can think about where you want to spend eternity. With this book, the road trip will be so much more enjoyable and we can make our world a better place to live in.

With that said, good reading and God bless you.

The Long and Winding Road
The Journey Begins

Chapter 1

The night I was beaten and left for dead makes for a dramatic story, but it wasn't the first time my life was at stake.

I was conceived in late 1959 or very early 1960. At that time, it was a shameful disgrace to be an unwed mother, which was my birthmother's case. She had to keep the pregnancy a secret from everyone in her hometown and at the Ohio college where she was a student. It was also a time that abortion was against the law. If desperate enough, women did find ways to get abortions, but many lost their lives in the process.

My birthmother chose to give birth to me, so I survived my first hurdle — I was born!

I was immediately put up for adoption and at the age of three weeks, I was adopted by a couple who could not have children naturally on their own. They had already adopted a boy who was two years old. He was happy to have a little sister.

I had a very good home and loving care. From very early on, I understood that I was special. My mother read a lot of books to me and one of them was about a couple who adopted a baby and how adoption happens and how happy they all were. For the first ten years or so, I thought every kid was adopted. Then I found out about the birds and the bees (sex) and realized that I was "different."

I asked myself what was wrong with me that my parents gave me away. I also always wondered whom I looked like and about my family history. At that time, adoptions were usually what is called "closed," where all people involved have no access to the other people's information. When I reached puberty, I really wanted to know more, but I couldn't get any answers.

I had an uneventful childhood, as normal as whatever "normal" is. I wasn't a very healthy child, though. I had a lot of allergies and if I caught a cold, it affected my stomach and I would throw up. And throw up a lot. I was quite a pro. At one point, world events seemed to mirror my inner physical turmoil. One evening in 1964, while I was watching television with my parents, the lampshade started to shake a little bit. None of us knew what it was, but the next day, we found out that there had been a devastating earthquake in Alaska. The quake killed hundreds of people and the tremors were felt as far away as the northern suburbs of Los Angeles, which is where we were. I was physically on shaky ground. Eventually, my mother had me tested and I started getting allergy shots when I was five years old. When I was seven, the doctor recommended that I have my tonsils and adenoids taken out.

As are many children, I was told before surgery to expect ice cream after waking up, but I was very disappointed. The anesthesia used in 1967 was not as advanced as it is today. It made me so sick that the force of my vomiting burst the tiny blood vessels in my face, which left little red dots all over my face. I never got to eat any ice cream before I was sent home.

Though my hospital visit was a difficult experience for me, it was nothing compared to what awaited me in the next couple of years.

I have had numerous times in my life that have turned from calm one minute to complete chaos the next. My first major experience with unexpected events occurred early in my eighth year. At four in the morning, I woke up to commotion in the house. Lights were on in the hallway and I heard voices. I got up to see what was going on and saw my dad lying on the floor, next to the bed in my parents' bedroom. My mother was trying to help him get up from the floor and he couldn't, as he was paralyzed.

About ten minutes later, the rescue squad arrived and ran into a problem. They were not able to load my dad on the stretcher and make the turn out of the bedroom into the living room to get him out. It took them about thirty minutes to get it done. He was taken to the hospital and put in intensive care; he'd had a severe stroke.

I remember at home, my mom had to clean the bedroom rug where my dad had had a bowel movement. He was trying to get out of bed to go to the bathroom when he had the stroke. My mom was never able to get the stain out.

My father was in the hospital for five months, making good progress each day. He got to the point where he was able to push a wheelchair down the hallway. Children weren't allowed to visit, so my mother had to sneak us in. I only saw my dad one time during the whole five months. It was scary for my brother and me, as my dad's face was paralyzed on one side and he looked spooky with the IVs hooked up and all.

Finally, in February 1969, the doctors decided my dad could come home. This was at the end of the fifth month and we made preparations. The day before he was to come home, the phone rang. I answered because my mom was asleep, but it was the hospital, so I woke her and she took the call. I watched as the look on her face changed to one of complete shock. Later, I learned that she'd been told, "your husband has expired."

Dad had been walking down the hallway in the unit and started to foam at the mouth and turn blue. They rushed to him and tried everything they could, but could not revive him. His aorta, which is the largest artery coming out of the

3

heart, had burst. There was no way they could have saved him.

That night, the house was full of people from our church and everyone was crying. It was so strange for me to see all these grown-ups who, all my young life, were the most stable people I knew, crying like babies. All they kept saying was, "He was so young." As a child, I didn't quite get it, as I felt he was old. All children think their parents are old.

That same year, my father's forty-two-year-old sister, my Aunt Mary, died after surgery for a stomach ulcer and then their mother, my grandmother, also died.

In the months after my father's death, my brother was very emotionally distraught and my mom didn't know how to handle him. It seemed that her health problems, real or imagined, took over her life. She became weak, depressed and unable to cope alone.

So, about six months after my dad died, my mom asked her only sister, who lived in New Jersey with her husband and two teenage sons, if she would take care of my brother and me for "a while" while my mom "recuperated." We lived in North Hollywood, California, so sending us to New Jersey was essentially sending us as far away as possible.

This would not be considered abuse or neglect in the traditional sense. But being uprooted and introduced into a family we didn't know and a new neighborhood and school system where we had no friends, so soon after our loss, was emotionally devastating to my brother and me. While living with my aunt and her family, I felt emotionally alone, having been shuffled away from home. Having to be the new kid in school in two different states, two different years, was not a very good experience.

Add to that my first encounter with a sexual predator, and you can see that it was not a good time for me. My girlfriend and I were walking home from school, when a man in a little red sports car pulled up next to us and said, "Hey girls, can you tell me where Party Street is?" Back in the 1960s, we were told not to take candy from strangers, but no one said to ignore them completely, so we walked a couple of steps over toward the car. I looked through the open window and saw that the man had his hands in his lap, holding his penis and moving it around.

My friend and I screamed and ran away. We went to her house and her mother called the police. They asked us a lot of questions and we were embarrassed about it. In hindsight, I see how close I'd come to being snatched, if that had been the man's intention.

We spent about one year in New Jersey, until late 1970. While we were gone, my mother said she was in the hospital because she was sick. She promised she would be better soon. We found out years later that she had been sent to a psychiatric hospital because there was nothing medically wrong with her. Depression's legitimacy was not as well recognized then as it is now, so patients were not treated with the same consideration they would receive today.

On February 9, 1971, a few months after we returned to California, I awoke to darkness. It was six o'clock in the morning and I thought I'd been dreaming that I was riding on a stagecoach in the "Wild West." In reality, my bed was scooting around the room! I ran to my mother's room and jumped into bed with her. My brother soon followed. We were all scared out of our minds.

There had been another earthquake and this one registered 6.6 on the Richter Scale, which is used to measure the strength of earth movement. The quake killed sixty-two people and injured hundreds of others. The next few days were terrible as the aftershocks kept coming, day and night. There was also the threat that the Van Norman Dam in the San Fernando Valley would break. Hundreds in the area had to be evacuated. Overpasses collapsed and buildings did, also.

> Fourteen persons were killed...nine of them in hospitals as a minute-long earthquake rolled over Los Angeles and suburbs at 6:02 a.m. It was the worst recorded quake in the city's history...Streets were strewn with shattered glass, concrete and bricks, walls buckled in major buildings, bridges cracked and some fell, freeways split, and thousands of homes suffered structural and internal destruction from tumbling furnishings..."I was virtually knocked out of bed," said a resident of a Los Angeles suburb. "When I got out I could barely walk the floor was rolling so"
>
> "Killer Quake," *Herald Examiner*, February 9, 1971.

About six months later, in September 1971, we moved to New Jersey. I was very happy, thinking I was getting away from earthquakes, but eventually, they caught up to me. There was a 3.9 quake in New Jersey when I was in school and I turned white as a sheet because I knew what it was, even though the other students didn't know at first. There was also one where I currently live in Virginia. It registered 4.5 and was quite strong for this area. It made news around here for days. It seems that wherever I go, I'm always on "shaky" ground, literally.

Chapter 2

Back in New Jersey, this time with our mother along, my brother and I went about building our new lives. As I entered my mid-teens, I didn't know who I was or what I wanted or had to do, except the usual things kids did, such as going to school. The biggest goal for everyone around that age was to "get out of school." In my free time, I hung out with some neighborhood kids and at one point, we heard that a fife and drum corps was forming. It was 1973 and the United States Bicentennial loomed on the horizon.

Six of my school friends and I attended the corps' first meetings and some of us thought the group sounded interesting. There was only one requirement. Each person who joined had to learn to play an instrument — either fife or drum — or had to be in the color guard. If you chose drums, you had the additional decision of bass versus snare.

I chose the fife, which is like a flute except of simpler construction. Simpler does not make it easier, however. In fact, it makes it much harder. The fife is just a tube of hollow wood — though our practice instruments were made of plastic — that has six holes drilled into it. There's another, bigger hole at one end that you blow across, as you might across the top of an open soda bottle.

My next-door neighbor and good friend, Gilbert, and I received our plastic fifes and sheet music and were told to teach ourselves to play. We were determined to learn and not only be good, but *really* good. This was the first time I seriously set a goal and worked toward achieving it. Gilbert and I drove the neighbors crazy because we practiced every day for months.

At the same time that I was having fun and working toward a worthy goal, I harbored an unhealthy secret. I entered puberty basically as a normal twelve and one-half-year-old girl. Most kids have insecurities of some sort and I was no different. When I started being attracted to boys, I was concerned, as are most girls, about the way I looked. I tried to dress nice — and I did — but I wasn't one of those kids who had "all they wanted," as my family was on a very limited income since my mother was the sole bread-winner and she was sick a lot of the time.

Fortunately, I was more the tomboy and, though I wanted to look nice, I wasn't really "into" clothes, as some girls were. My mom bought what I needed and once a year, I got to pick out some things I especially wanted so I could keep in style.

It was during this time that I started to baby-sit every week. I had my own bank account and I loved to watch it grow, so I worked as much as I could. Because we didn't have a large income, food was a consideration at my house and we didn't have any extras *at all*. When I baby-sat, I saw how other people ate and what kinds of food they had. It was so tempting that I couldn't help but try some of it. It was really good and soon I realized I was putting on weight.

At some point, I realized that I could eat what I wanted, remember what order I ate it in, and then when I had satis-fied my cravings, I could "solve" the guilt of having eaten the food by vomiting it up. I did this until the first items I ate came out, which meant that all of the "bad" food was gone and I wouldn't gain weight. In the early 1970s, there was not widespread knowledge about this practice; I just figured it out and it worked.

I didn't know it then, but what I was doing was called bingeing and purging. I continued doing it an average of twice a week for four years, until I got a job at a fast food place. There, I was too busy to think of eating while I worked and so for about the next five years, I only vomited when I binged on "naughty" goodies. In years since, the habit of bingeing and purging has been identified as a medical condition known as bulimia.

A sort of "sister" condition is anorexia, which involves severely and unhealthily limiting what one consumes. At times, I simply didn't eat, sometimes for up to four days.

Also during my adolescence, I experienced my second hospital stay. The fife and drum corps practices and school went well, and school kept me busy until the fall of 1974. Late one night when my mother returned from a date, her boyfriend at the time ended up taking me to the hospital, where I was admitted for an appendectomy. My mother couldn't drive me because she was on crutches, recovering from a broken hip, but she didn't even ride along. In fact, she didn't visit me even once during my weeklong stay because she didn't have the "energy" to do so.

I was fortunate that my eating disorders didn't get so bad that they interfered with my ability to pursue goals. In 1975, when I was fourteen years old, I participated in a teen art show and photos of two of my paintings appeared in the local newspaper.

I also continued to play the fife and by 1976, the group I was in had become the official fife and drum corps for the national battlefield in our area. We had about thirty members and traveled to ten out of the thirteen original colonies to play in parades that were held almost every weekend, throughout the spring and summer months. We even were invited to play in the 1976 Macy's Day Parade in New York City and appear on a daytime television show.

In July, state fife and drum corps competitions took place across the nation. Our corps, The Battle of Monmouth Ancient Fife and Drum Corp, won second place in New Jersey. Gilbert won for best male fifer in the state and

I won for third best female fifer. I had not entered myself in the competition but the leaders entered me when we arrived there, and so with no practice I had to play, and I guess I did well. It was a thrill and an honor to be a state champ on our country's 200th birthday and the timing was extra-special for me, as I would soon turn Sweet 16.

Daniel Savino (left) in corps uniform and Mrs. Margaret Weber, the group's business manager, look on as Richard Barker, Superintendent of Monmouth Battlefield State Park, directs a

Liberty Tree planting on Cobb House lawn. Joel Holmes with shovel, with Gail and Lynn Jakelis (right foreground).

"Liberty Tree Planting Day," *Asbury Park Press*, April 17, 1976.

"THE LIBERTY TREE"
Original poem by MARY ANN KARL

Back in the beginning of the USA, it was very very different than it is today. There were thirteen little colonies all under British care, the odds were all against us but we fought for what was fair.

It happened so surprisingly, it shocked the entire globe, we won our independence, but it's cause we still must probe.

It started with some farmers, from all across the land, the spirit got them moving, everybody gave a hand.

The spirit moved inside them, it made them brave and strong, they fought with all their courage and they sang a liberty song.

This song was truly a good one, it told of a liberty tree which stood for all their hopes and dreams, of what America could be.

That's why we plan to plant a tree, it's to remind us of our past, of all the good that life can bring and to try and make it last.

The past two hundred years have shown all that we can do, and the spirit like the tree we plant really comes from me and you.

Shortly after this, I started to concentrate more on my artwork, an interest I'd held since kindergarten. In my senior year of high school, I set a goal to do my best artwork; I entered contests and won a few of them.

Asbury Park Press

TEEN ARTS FESTIVAL — Joan Luckhardt of Little Silver, co-chairman of the Monmouth County Teen Arts Festival admires one of the paintings being displayed in the show that opened yesterday at the Monmouth Mall. Exhibits in painting, photography and sculpture done by elementary and high school students in Monmouth County will be on display through Saturday. Professional demonstrations and student performances of plays, dance, and poetry readings will held today through Thursday. All students performances are scheduled between 10 a.m. and 2 p.m. and are open to the public.

"Teen Arts Festival," *Asbury Park Press*, April 1975.

Not surprisingly, artwork wasn't my only interest at that age. As an average teenage girl, I had the usual crushes and such on boys. Unfortunately, since my father's death, there had been no steady male influence in my home, no example of what a healthy male-female relationship should look like, no male standard against which I could measure the boys who interested me.

At sixteen, I started dating a boy named John Warmouth, whom I knew from biology class the previous year.

It was during that class that he was joking around and threw a lead pipe at me, almost hitting me in the head! While it's true that when a boy of that age likes a girl, he may try to get the girl's attention in some outlandish ways, that was a bit much for a simple attention-getter. Too bad I didn't think about that at the time; twenty years later, the irony of that moment would haunt me.

John and I started dating steadily in 1977. Perhaps wanting to fill the void left by my father's death and the void of wanting security in my life since my mother was always sick, and perhaps wanting to fulfill the "American dream" of a house with a white picket fence, two kids and a dog, I ignored some of the warning signs that John wasn't the perfect mate for me — possibly not for anyone — and focused on the fact that he came from a solid, middle-class family and was a good prospect, so to speak.

Having addressed and at least partially achieved my goal of doing my best artwork, and thinking I had my romantic future fairly well in hand, I set my sights on other grown-up endeavors, such as attending college to earn first, an associate's degree and then, a bachelor's degree. Even at that age, when I set my mind on something, I didn't want to do it partly or halfway. I wanted to see it through and to this day, I still do. That combination of effort and determination is a reflection of who I am and you can make it your legacy, too.

The summer of 1980 was eventful in many respects. That hot, hot August really gave meaning to the saying "the dog days of summer." The air was so stifling and the mood at home was the same. I felt that I was being smothered. As I tried to stretch my wings of independence, my mother got more and more afraid of losing me. It was one hot August night when I was sitting on the front porch of my house that my best male friend Gilbert came over. He asked if I was busy, as he wanted to talk about something very serious and he felt it was at a point of being a crisis. I told him that I always had time for him.

Ever since our early teens when we started practicing for the fife and drum corps every day we had developed a really deep friendship. I was considered by all the kids in school to be one of the lucky ones. You see, Gilbert was the most popular guy in high school. He was not only very good looking but he was really nice and a gentleman. All the girls wanted to date him, including me. He did not try to get them right into the sack, so to speak, which was the thing to do during the late 1970s. I had a crush on him for a while, but we were such good friends and we just never "dated" like he did with other more "popular" girls. One of those girls, who I disliked so much at the time because she was his girlfriend, was a girl named Debbie. When they broke up she and I became really good friends.

So to start the conversation that night, he said that since we were both out of school he felt it would be the right time to ask my advice since he valued my friendship so much. What he told me left me speechless. He said that the mailman who delivered our mail would come over every day, and through the last year the mailman started to say things to Gilbert that had a sexual meaning to them. After a while they developed a friendship that then progressed to the point where they became sexually intimate. Gilbert then said, with some quiet pauses, as he tried to feel out my reactions in the darkness, that he was gay.

With that said he wanted to know if I hated him. I was surprised that he even asked that question, but I understood how he would fear rejection from anyone who knew this "secret" that he had been keeping for years. I told him that what he did in the bedroom was not going to determine my love for him the person. I could tell that he instantly felt a sense of relief like a weight had been lifted off his shoulder.

The next few weeks we talked about it a lot and being honest with him I told him that while it did make me feel grossed out thinking about the act itself, it was something that every person chooses for themselves, and they have to live with that decision. I did not love him any less. Looking back at his popularity in school with the girls it all made more sense. He was not trying to get them in the sack and was a gentleman because he did not want to have sex with girls. Being his best friend all those years, I would have thought that I would have picked up on something to clue me in to his sexual orientation, but nothing did. He was such a kind, caring person and we really were close.

He then asked me if I would be willing to do something that would help him feel better socially. He knew that I was good friends with Debbie, his old girlfriend. He asked if Debbie and I would go out with his boyfriend and him for dinner, and this way we could meet the guy. We were not sure at first but decided to go. It was quite fun as to the whole night. To anyone else it looked like a double date. Two guys and two girls. But we all knew who was with whom. It was rather strange. That night was just about the last time we saw Gilbert. He came over to my house and told my mother and me that he had changed his name to Mario, moved into a house with a group of other gay guys and he was planning to move to New York City.

By the end of that hot, stifling summer, when I was almost twenty, I moved out of my mother's house to rent an apartment with my now best friend, Debbie, whom I had known since early in high school. Only three months after I moved in with Debbie, my mother broke her hip and wanted me to return home to care for her. She tried to make me feel guilty, but I didn't move back in — I merely added daily visits to attend to her physical and emotional needs to my already busy school and work schedule. I attended an all-girl, Catholic college so I wouldn't expose myself to too much coed guy stuff. I thought this would help my chances with John. Even so, I did go to a lot of bars with Debbie during this time, so I would have the chance to experience other situations with guys and know if I was attracted to anyone else.

Honesty was very important to me, as well as my determination to keep my virginity until marriage. I didn't want to do anything to ruin my chances for a "perfect" and lifelong marriage, because my mother had drilled it into my head that divorce was something only "bad" people did.

My mother had started to date a few years after my dad passed away and that was when I first heard about "being divorced." It was explained to me that being widowed was somehow "noble," but being divorced meant there was something wrong with the person because the marriage didn't work. I guess I had that in my mind all through my teens, because when I found what I thought was the perfect "all-American" boy to date, I made sure I did everything right, so to speak. I dated no one else at all and led the relationship in the direction we both thought would work out the way we planned.

While living with Debbie, I supported myself on a monthly check from Social Security that I received because of my father's death. It was mine as long as I went to college full time and maintained a B average. However, it wasn't enough to make ends meet, so I had to work full time during the summers.

Right before getting married to John, the news broke that doctors had discovered a new disease called AIDS. It was incurable and mostly struck gay men. Debbie and I worried about Gilbert because his lifestyle was very secretive and did not keep him safe from this killer. We learned that he did contract AIDS (Gilbert died of AIDS in 1995).

Debbie didn't want to go to college and so worked various jobs, mostly secretarial. In 1980, she was working for a company that drilled for oil. The office where she worked needed more help since business was doing so well, so Debbie asked me if I wanted to work there for the summer. I had graduated with an associate's degree the previous year and was pursuing a bachelor's degree, so I hadn't started a full-time job and jumped at the chance to have one, temporarily. After working in the accounting department for about three weeks and being in charge of disbursing shareholder dividends, I saw how much money the company's investors were being paid on their stock.

One day, the boss asked Debbie and me to help him with an upcoming presentation he was going to give in New York City for future investors and company executives. Debbie prepared numerous written handouts and I created visual aids the boss would use during his speech, including two-by-three-foot posters that explained exactly what went on in the drilling process and boasted the company's logo. The presentation was held on the 102nd floor in the World Trade Center, right in the heart of the business world. Debbie and I were excited to have this opportunity.

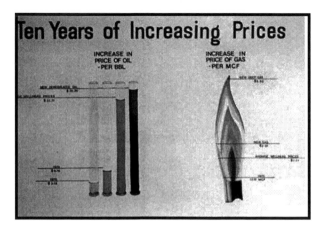

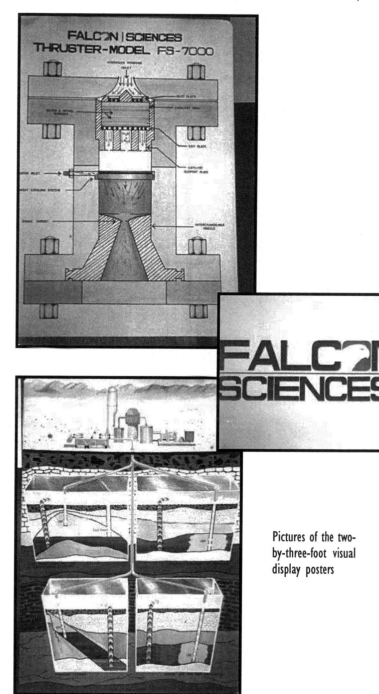

Pictures of the two-by-three-foot visual display posters

When we returned home, we told Debbie's parents and relatives and my mother about our experience and how much money we could make. We all bought stock in the company. I even invested the college fund that my paternal grandmother had left to me.

About two months later, the bottom fell out! The man who "owned" the company was a fraud! He'd made up the whole thing to get peoples' investment dollars. Debbie and I talked to other employees who filled us in on some little bits of information and we found out that the Securities and Exchange Commission was looking for him and had been for a long time.

Desperate because I was about to lose my whole college fund, which I needed so I could pay off my college loans, I confronted the boss and threatened to reveal his identity to the SEC if he didn't return Debbie's parents' and my money, as well as that of our family members. Within a week, the money was secretly returned to all of us.

Debbie and I reported him to the SEC, anyway. Come to find out, the man had a history of fraud and scams like that. Fraud is still alive and well today and scammers have become much more sophisticated. To read more about what fraud is, how to recognize it, and what to do when you've identified it somewhere, refer to this book's Resource Guide and Information.

When I think of how dangerous our boss was and how I confronted him, I am still amazed at my behavior. Too bad I didn't have that same courage in the early years of my relationship with my future husband.

Former area man remains fugitive

By KIRK MOORE
Press Toms River Bureau

THE SMALL TOWN of Smyrna, Del., is where fugitive stock dealer Christos Netelkos set up shop after violating parole in 1984, according to federal officials who are investigating the convicted swindler's dealings over the past year.

At 56 W. Commerce St., the home office of Worldmasters Corp., lawyers for the federal government and business people who have a share in court judgements against Netelkos have come to examine assets that were frozen by federal court order last week.

The former Toms River resident was arrested Jan. 8 in Denver, Colo., as he was selling stock in his company at a Denver brokerage house. The federal Securities and Exchange Commission traced Netelkos' business to Smyrna, a town of about 4,500 people situated 10 miles north of Dover, Del.

According to a SEC complaint filed in federal court in Wilmington, Del., last Wednesday, Netelkos used the alias Frank W. Roland in his new life as president of Worldmasters Corp.

"It's like a Harry Houdini story," said Eugene G. Liss, federal marshal for New Jersey.

The SEC charges the prospectus for Worldmasters stock failed to disclose that its president and chief shareholder was really Netelkos, convicted in a 1970s stock fraud that brought about the collapse of

the New Jersey brokerage house Christian-Paine & Co., Inc.

Netelkos was freed after serving three years of an 11-year sentence for his role in stealing millions of dollars from Christian-Paine investors. In 1984 a federal court entered a $3.4 million judgement against Netelkos and two of his confederates who sold nearly seven million shares of phony stock in Falcon Sciences, Inc., a Colts Neck-based firm created for the legitimate development of petroleum technology.

Netelkos dropped out of sight in the summer of 1984, after a federal judge cited him for contempt when he transferred Falcon Sciences oil leases into his own account in defiance of a court order.

A second warrant for his arrest was issued when he failed to show up for a September 1984 parole hearing.

The SEC believes Netelkos was back in business the following year, with the creation of Worldmasters Corp. to sell computer software and programming to business users.

Michael D. Donovan, a staff attorney with the SEC regional office in Arlington, Va., said Worldmasters stock sales raised at least $75,000 since Sept. 11, 1985.

"As far as we can tell, they have about 135 shareholders," Donovan said.

At a Thursday court hearing, a temporary restraining order was issued, freezing Worldmasters' assets, Donovan said. He would not comment on what assets have been seized.

CHRISTOS NETELKOS
Like a Houdini story

Netelkos employed a number of Delaware residents in his business, but Donovan said they apparently believed they were working for a legitimate businessman.

"They appeared to think he was Frank Roland," he said.

Falcon Sciences was created to develop new petroleum and natural gas production technology.

Through their secret control of the company, Netelkos and Charles Gamarekian, of Sparta, were able to issue nearly seven million shares of unauthorized and probably counterfeit stock during 1982 and 1983, according to a judgment issued in 1984 by U.S. District Court Judge Shirley Wohl Krom.

With the help of Arno Arndt, a confederate working in Europe, Netelkos and Gamarekian were able to sell three million shares through the Swiss branches of American brokerage houses.

News article about my boss the crook.
Press Toms River Bureau, Kirk Moore, "Former Area Man Remains Fugitive," appeared in *Asbury Park Press,* January, 1985.

When I think of how dangerous our boss was and how I confronted him, I am still amazed at my behavior. Too bad I didn't have that same courage in the early years of my relationship with my future husband.

During the five and one-half years that John and I dated, he was sometimes emotionally cold. Once, when I pushed him to express himself, he punched the wall in the apartment in frustration. It scared me, but I brushed it off at the time. John was also very cold to Debbie. She dated a couple of guys and I think he felt she was a threat to my relationship with him because I might decide to date someone else, as she did. At times, John was very cruel and sarcastic, but he was also young and fun. I thought he would mature and, overall, he was a hard worker, so I thought that with time, we would make a good couple.

John and me in 1977 going to our junior year high school prom.

Chapter 3

I earned my bachelor of art degree in May 1982 and that August, John and I got married. We planned to wait a while to start a family, so we both worked and settled into our marriage. In some ways, nothing had changed. During our marriage, the biggest problem was that John would criticize me in public, saying things such as, "Oh, she can't cook like she should."

I knew he wasn't saying the truth and I brushed off his comments, blaming his inability to compliment me on his lack of maturity. When we started dating in high school, that was how he kidded around and I figured he hadn't grown up, yet. As it turned out, the problem went beyond immaturity. John's criticism was constant, especially in public with friends, and it went on for years.

About a year into our marriage, I had just gotten a new job. We were still having protected sexual relations because we weren't ready for a family. We were always careful, but one afternoon we were engaging in foreplay and things went a little too far. We were close to going "all the way" and just before John entered me, I stopped him, telling him it was too close to the middle of my cycle to not use a condom. We stopped and he put one on3, and he did not ejaculate inside me, as I did not trust condoms during my most fertile time. About two weeks later I was due to get my period, but I didn't. Another week went by and I started to wonder if I were pregnant. My breasts ached and I was nauseous. It appeared that I had the classic pregnancy symptoms, but how could that be? I hadn't had intercourse.

Home pregnancy tests had come out, but weren't advertised on TV; in general, the public wasn't aware of them. Instead, the next day, I called to make an appointment with my obstetrician/gynecologist for an exam and pregnancy test. The soonest appointment I could get was three weeks later.

I finally had my appointment and the next day, when I was to get called with the results from the test, I went to work. About an hour after arriving, I went to the bathroom and I found out I was bleeding! I wondered if I was just getting my period really late.

That afternoon when I got home, I received the call from the doctor's office and they told me that I was, indeed, pregnant. Then I told them that I was bleeding really heavily, to the point that blood was just dripping like a faucet. They said to collect everything that was coming out and put it in a jar and if the bleeding didn't stop in an hour, I was to call them and go to the emergency room.

I did as they said, which was really quite gross. I had a spoon and I had to let the blood drip into the jar and catch the clots with a spoon and put them there, too.

When John came home from work, he called the doctor's office and we went to the emergency room and turned over the jar of blood and tissue I'd collected. The doctor said I was having a miscarriage and he needed to do a D&C — dilatation and curettage. This is where the doctor dilates the cervix and scrapes the inside of the uterus to clean it out. The bleeding would stop and the miscarriage would be "complete." I spent the night in the hospital and then stayed home from work for a week. Five weeks later, I had an appointment with the doctor and he said I was okay, physically. A lab report showed that I had started my third month of pregnancy when the

miscarriage occurred. It also showed there were "no iden-
tifiable body parts!"

I couldn't believe such plain words were used to describe such a devastating experience. The doctor was very
cold and uncaring, as though he read from a report about
my car being checked by a mechanic. Needless to say, I was
emotionally thrown from one end of the spectrum to the
other — life and then the death of a baby.

Besides sending me on an emotional roller coaster ride,
my pregnancy and miscarriage also rekindled my interest in
finding my birthparents. I had never abandoned my desire,
but as a child, I really couldn't do much, and as a young
adult, I had been busy working, attending college and starting my marriage.

Again, external events seemed to echo my internal experience. Not long after I suffered the loss of my baby, our
community suffered a loss when a fire destroyed a historic
racetrack. It burned so hot and was so close to my home
that everyone in the neighborhood had to hose down their
roofs with water to keep the embers from catching them
on fire. We had to go without electricity and water for over
a week, and the whole town was devastated by this event.
When life got back to normal, John and I decided to try and
start a family as I thought I would be very fertile for some
unknown reason, just a gut feeling.

Sure enough on our first try, I got pregnant again and
my son Matthew was born in 1985. I had to have an unplanned Caesarian section after being in labor for twen-
ty-seven hours. It was an especially traumatic experience
because the epidural used for pain relief hadn't worked
properly. It only gave me relief on the right side of my body
and when I was taken in for surgery, I had what is called a
"window" — in other words, no anesthesia — on the left
side of my body! I screamed at them and told them what
they were doing.

This picture was taken right in front of my house and it shows how close the fire was.

The historic raceway that burned down.

"You are cutting through my muscles; you are retracting them." When I said, "You are cutting my uterus," they knew I had no anesthesia and slapped a gas mask on my face that delivered enough anesthesia to knock me out.

I awoke to find that I was hemorrhaging, which they stopped by putting a bag of ice on my newly cut abdomen — a very painful and horrible introduction to motherhood. That crisis pushed me into planning my next birth very carefully, a process that took the next year and a half.

In the meantime, I started a very serious search for my birthparents in 1986. I joined any group available that might assist me and wrote many letters to Oprah, whose show was doing lots of birthparent-adopted child reunions in those days. I never received a reply from the Oprah show and, even with the knowledge and resources I gained from my groups, the going was slow.

In 1987, my second son, Michael, was born. After forty-two hours of labor, my cervix still hadn't dilated past eight centimeters and the baby could not progress through the birth canal. Despite all the effort I'd made to find a doctor and hospital that wouldn't force me to have a C-section just because I'd already had one (a common practice at that time), I had to have a C-section to deliver Michael.

After having both of my children, I lost all the weight I had gained, which was a lot! Between them I had gained one hundred and fourteen pounds. Also, Matthew was a big baby, weighing ten pounds and measuring twenty-three inches in length. I had stretched so much with him that I had torn my abdominal muscles, which caused them to herniate. The more I did sit-ups to tone them, the more they stuck out; I knew something was terribly wrong.

I was left with a large amount of extra skin that didn't go away. My skin's not very elastic, so what stretched stayed that way. I felt I was too young to be left with this "mess" on me, but I couldn't fix it myself. I did my homework and found a plastic surgeon that could fix my hernia and repair the damage. In 1989 when Michael was a year and five months old, I had it done. It was my first experience with what you see now on the reality television shows such as *Extreme Makeover* and *Plastic Surgery—Before & After*.

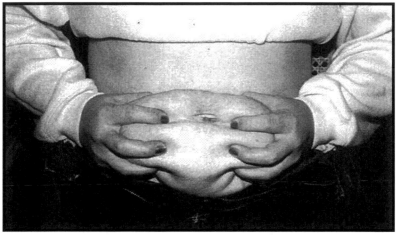

I lost all the weight from the pregnancies, but the skin was so stretched.

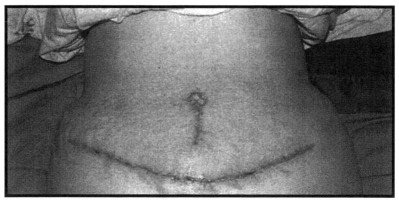

The scars from the surgery. They faded after a couple of years.

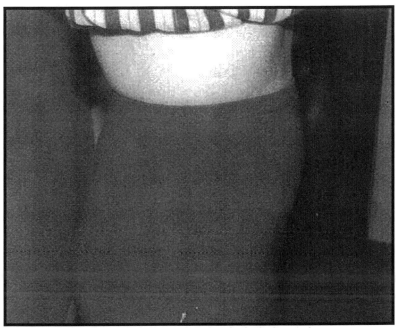

After the repair, I was so pleased to be back the way I was.

This was my first surgery where I was able to choose my surgeon. Previous procedures were done when I was a child and had no say, or when I had the D&C and C-sections, which my OB/GYN performed. Not that he wasn't my doctor of choice, only that he was already treating me and so did the necessary, unplanned surgeries, rather than my planning ahead and choosing a surgeon based on research. Through this process and others for future surgeries, I learned quite a bit about choosing a doctor and other support and rehabilitative services. One very important thing I learned is that if you are having cosmetic surgery, you should be sure your surgeon is board certified.

Chapter 4

Seven years into my marriage, I was still hoping that John would mature and start treating me with more kindness and respect. But as I've said, it turns out that immaturity was not the main problem. I later learned that a tendency to abuse others can stem from low self-esteem and a need to exert control. The feeling of a lack of control can also cause frustration, which may result in lashing out and inappropriately physical solutions to perceived problems.

Things got worse after the children were born. John thought they should be perfect; he was the boss and they should behave. If the children misbehaved, John's anger would surface and boil to the point that I had to step in and calm him down. It was as though John was a military drill instructor and the boys were in basic training.

It's one thing to be a firm parent, but you must also show affection. John rarely did and I had to compensate for that by making sure the boys knew they were loved and okay. Also, Matthew was diagnosed with ADHD (attention deficit hyperactivity disorder), which aggravated the problems.

One incident that occurred in 1990 while John and I still lived in New Jersey, was in hindsight a red flag for just how vindictive and angry my husband could be. Our family shared a backyard, separated by a chain link fence with a gate in it, with my next-door neighbor and good friend, Sheree, and her family. Sheree had her feelings hurt that she and her five kids weren't invited to a birthday party I held for Matthew a few weeks earlier. I hadn't invited her because she was strapped for money and I didn't want her to feel as though she needed to buy a gift for my son.

I told John that Sheree was upset with me and he did something I couldn't believe. He went into the backyard with his welder and welded the gate between our yards shut! It was as though he took personal offense to a minor upset between my friend and me. He had gone too far. I had to talk to Sheree and her husband, Dave, to make amends and also get John to apologize for his actions.

My friendship with Sheree survived the incident and our children continued to play together. The next year, when Matthew was five, he was playing next door with Sheree's children and ran into the corner of the fence. When Sheree brought Matthew into the house and I looked at his eye, I knew something was seriously wrong. Something black was sticking out of the white of his eye.

Sheree called 911 and while waiting for the ambulance, I remained calm for my son's sake. Then, on the way to the hospital, the ambulance caught fire! The back of the ambulance filled with smoke and we were unable to get to the hospital entrance. We had to wheel Matthew on a stretcher about an eighth of a mile up the driveway to the emergency room.

Matthew was diagnosed with a popped eyeball and required surgery. The black I'd seen was his iris (the colored part of the eye) coming out of the sclera (the white of the eye). Today, Matthew's vision is really good at 20/40 in that eye, and the only thing you notice is that his iris looks like a cat's eye instead of round, as it should.

Later in 1990, John was laid off from his job as a union glazer, which is someone who installs glass windows in new buildings. We didn't have any income except for odd jobs that he could find. With a mortgage and the usual bills to pay and no income, we were on the verge of losing our home. We decided to sell. We finally got an offer from someone to buy our house, but at a much lower price than it was worth. However, we were desperate at that point, so we accepted the offer.

Unfortunately, it wasn't that easy. As part of the inspection process, we had to test our house for Radon, a radioactive gas formed naturally in the ground. It occurs in many areas in the country and was found to exist in our home at way above the acceptable level. The level was equal to the exposure of smoking two packs of cigarettes a day. We had to install a system to vent the gas out of our basement so we could sell our home.

With that settled, we went to Virginia, where John's sister, Kathy, lived. We loved it there because it was still very much the country. In New Jersey during the 1980s, it had gotten so crowded that we'd wanted to get out of there and now was the time.

We found a house within our price range, but we also had to take my disabled mother with us; she didn't want to be left alone in New Jersey. My brother lived there, but he had never helped her when she had been sick or injured because I lived closer and, as the daughter, I was the natural choice to see to all of her grocery shopping, housework and physical care.

Since we were trying to save money on the move, we rented a U-Haul truck. With the help of my brother, sister-in-law, and nephews, we spent eight hours loading it. We were to spend the night with my in-laws, who lived across town, because we had to leave the next morning to close on the new house in Virginia.

My sons and I took the car to my in-laws' house, which was about ten minutes away. John was to follow in the rental truck. When he didn't arrive in fifteen minutes, I couldn't understand it; he had been right behind us when we left the old house.

I got back in the car and re-traced my route. To my horror, I came upon the moving truck that, along with our belongings, was being hosed down by firefighters. An eighteen-year-old girl had pulled out in front of John and both vehicles were totaled in the collision. That meant we had to hire a professional moving company to unload the totaled U-Haul truck and reload it into their truck and get it down to Virginia as soon as possible. We couldn't afford that, so my mother-in-law paid for it.

To already be under the pressure of a move and have that happen was really a mess. We did close on the house the next day, but had to sleep on pillows and blankets we borrowed from Kathy for the first three nights. Maybe it was a sign that my life in Virginia was not going to be easy.

About a year later, we were settled into our neighborhood and things were going fine. Then one day, my younger son, Michael, was playing in the woods with Sheree and her kids, who were visiting from New Jersey. I heard horrible screams and then Matthew and Sheree's daughter Joy came running into the house and said that Michael and Sheree's son, Bobby, who are the same age, were covered with bees! John ran into the woods and swatted at the bees and dragged both boys back to the house.

I kept the older kids calm and when the younger boys got to the house, John and I picked bees out of the boys' noses, ears and hair. Then Sheree and I put them in the car and sped to the hospital. In the country it takes longer to wait for an ambulance to come, and with the chance of a serious allergic reaction, we couldn't wait. We counted twenty-eight stings on Michael and Bobby had about

Through the years from the outside, things looked picture perfect.

the same. He swelled up more than Michael, but both boys received antihistamines to stop further swelling. They were okay for the rest of the visit, but to this day, they don't like bees or other stinging insects. I can understand why.

I started to work part-time jobs during the first year we lived in Virginia, as did John. But in 1992, sometime after the bee incident, while moving a mattress from one room to another, I ruptured a disc in my lower back. I lay at home, flat on my back, for two weeks. Finally, I saw an orthopedic doctor who admitted me directly from his office into the hospital across the street. He did emergency surgery the next morning at six-thirty.

I was frantic, as I didn't know who was going to take care of the boys. John had just gotten a new job and my mother wasn't really able to handle them, as they were lively four- and six-year-olds. It was the help of women from a club I belonged to that got us through. The club was a civic group that helped the local community with its needs, such as fire victims and needy families. I just happened to be a new member and now I was on the receiving end. They really practiced what they preached. They brought me hot meals and watched the boys, etc.

It was about a year later that Nancy, one of the women in the club, heard that I was in need of a job during the boys' school hours. She told me that her husband needed a receptionist to work during school hours because he was trying to run his business alone. I immediately called her husband to set up a time to meet him for an interview. John and I were in desperate need of money, like most young families, but we also needed to build an in-law apartment onto our house for my mother.

I started my new job in March 1993. I was a bit uncomfortable at first because, like most people, I had never been at a funeral home — the business that Nancy's husband Matt owned — except for visitations and funerals. But after a few months there, I realized it was the thing I had dreamed of doing with my life all along.

I recalled when my mother's mother passed away when I was in my late twenties. Her visitation was such a peaceful evening. I had seen her two days before in the hospital when she was dying and she had looked terrible. When I saw her in the casket, she looked better than she had in almost twenty years! I was amazed at how good and at peace she seemed. I had the first feeling of curious interest, wondering, "how could they do that?" It didn't occur to me that someday I'd know every detail.

I felt that God had opened a window when I got the job during school hours, but I faced the first summer of having to put the boys in childcare. To make things worse, I had to use my whole paycheck to pay for that and ended up making only fifty-two cents a week that first summer, after paying for the boys' care.

I decided that the funeral business took all of my talents — having worked as a medical claims examiner for an insurance company, having a degree in fine art and minors in psychology and sociology, and being a people person — and rolled them all into one. Taking care of the family of the deceased is an honor, but a lot goes into it. There's a small amount of office work and you must use medical and artistic skills to have the deceased look as good as possible. You also work with the public. I felt that this was God opening a door for me, but I needed to work full time year-round so I wouldn't make fifty-two cents per week every summer.

I asked Matt if I could *please* do what was required to get my license. That involved an eighteen-month internship and also a two-year degree in funeral service. My boss desperately needed the help, as he was the owner and I was the only employee, other than an older gentleman who helped transport flowers and vehicles during funerals. Matt saw how well I worked with the public and decided I would make a good addition to the business, since he was the only licensed person at the funeral home and no one else could embalm the bodies if he were sick.

In April 1994, Matt agreed to my request and I started my internship and going to college. I applied to the only funeral college in the state of Virginia, which was thirty-five miles from home. The commute would take me about forty-five minutes to class each day and it would be tough, but we coordinated my school schedule with work. In fall 1994, I scheduled twenty-one college credits. That was double the full-time course load, but it would enable me to graduate the next spring.

During that time, I saw some of the most heartbreaking, real-life experiences that some of us will have to go through. They involved cases such as when my boss and I had to go to an automobile accident scene to pick up someone who was killed in the crash. I really felt the presence of the person, as if he were still there, as if his spirit still lingered near him.

One very sad time was when an eighteen-year-old boy shot himself in the head. We had to reconstruct his head so the family could have an open casket for the funeral.

The saddest cases were once, when I went to the morgue to pick up a stillborn infant and, another time, a little girl just under the age of one. Being a mother, myself, and carrying them in my arms was so personal that it really affected me. I realized that what I was doing was not just a "job," it was something I felt I *needed* to be doing.

So, I learned at work what I was being taught at school. I had to reconstruct the body of someone who'd been autopsied, which required a lot of intricate replacement of the body's organs and stitching the body closed again. It was the application of some of the techniques I learned in my restorative art class. That was where we learned how to reconstruct a human who has been damaged by disease, surgery, autopsy or trauma. We also learned how to use color for the makeup and most importantly, how to use wax and other materials to build body parts that may have been ripped off, torn, surgically removed or otherwise accidentally destroyed.

In that class, the instructor asked me to be co-instructor due to the skills I had from my fine art degree, from which I knew how to sculpt. In the restorative art class, we learned that each human head is exactly the same in the basic measurements, such as the distance between the eyes, nose, and ears, etc. I helped my classmates make noses, ears, and eyes, and showed them how to attach real hair to the heads and how to use the right type of make-up.

Other classes required for the degree were similar to those for becoming a doctor. They included chemistry, Anatomy I and II, pathology, and microbiology. Additionally, I studied embalming, funeral history, business management, accounting, speech communication, psychology of death and dying, and grief counseling.

Chapter 5

As I pursued my education and new career, John's abuse of the kids and me continued at home. To some extent, emotional abuse is much worse than physical abuse because it leaves no outer signs that others can see. I didn't let John's criticism damage my self-esteem because I knew that what I did was as good as or better than what most wives or my other girlfriends were doing. But it did create a deep, inner longing in my soul for praise or compliments, which were never given.

After thirteen years of marriage, I felt as though we were two strangers living in the same house. But no matter how much I tried to get John to talk to me or share his feelings, he would clam up. He would leave me crying and on another day, I would ask him if we could work on our marriage and his comment would be, "Oh, you are bringing that crap up again!"

When I'd worked at the funeral home for two years, Matt, having seen how abused I was, took advantage of the situation. I was so emotionally vulnerable that I didn't know how to handle what was about to happen. It was January 5, 1995, and I had already served nine months of my internship. That morning, I had to take my mother to the hospital for surgery on her knee, which she had broken a few months previous; I would have to pick her up that afternoon.

I went to work and at about ten o'clock, we received a death call. I returned to the hospital, went to the morgue, and picked up the gentleman who had died, then took him back to the funeral home. Matt and I started to work on him and about three hours later, we got another call that a woman had died. She was brought to the funeral home for us by a service that we used when we couldn't pick up the person ourselves. By about six that evening, Matt let me go home and make dinner; I told him I would be back about nine o'clock, once I picked up my mother from the hospital and got her settled. Once I'd done this, I kissed her good-night and left to go back to work.

When I arrived, Matt was at the back door and he opened it for me. He looked very tired, as I was, but we went right to work.

As we worked on the gentleman's body, Matt asked, "Can I trust you?"

Eager to be a good employee and since we were some-what friends, due to my acquaintance with his wife and my employment with him for almost two years, I replied, "Of course you can. What's the matter?"

He said he wanted to know if he could trust me with his personal feelings and then proceeded to tell me that I was the best thing that had happened to his funeral business, as the public really seemed to like a woman funeral director. Then he said that I was the best thing to happen to him, personally!

That just stopped me dead in my tracks. I didn't know what to make of what he said. I never would have thought he could mean "personally" to mean really *personally,* but he did. I was really speechless. If he were crude, vulgar, or outright ugly, I could have just ignored him. But because he was my boss, first and foremost, and we were friends, also, I was really upset. I had never ever imagined that he, of all people, could mean what he said as anything but a compliment, but I felt it was more than that. Matt was married, had three children, and was a deacon in one of the largest churches in the county. His father was a Baptist preacher who did funerals for us when asked.

We finished embalming that night and I went home, but I couldn't sleep much at all. I felt sick inside and my fears were confirmed the next day when Matt's conversation turned to the point where it sort of left off the previous night. He wanted more than just a working relationship with me and he started to quote scripture from the Bible!

You must understand that this was done in such a way and I was under so much pressure that, emotionally, I was unable to fend him off. At home, I was being emotionally abused and pushed away by my husband and now, at work, I was being subjected to hours of what I now call biblical brainwashing conversation that made it unbearably stressful. What he did is called emotional rape. Nothing happened for over two weeks, but Matt's emotional pressure took its toll. I let him get physical. The biggest problem I faced was that I had nowhere to turn. I couldn't talk to anyone about the situation because in small towns, gossip is rampant and I couldn't trust anyone. I couldn't quit my job because everyone knew I loved it and was going to college to get my license. They would ask why I'd left. Lastly, I couldn't report his behavior to someone higher up in the chain of command because he was the top.

As time went on, it was like every time Matt made an advance, I was unable to fend him off due to my emotional need for approval, which my husband should have been giving me, but was not. Sometimes I tried to stop Matt's advances and he would tell me that Jesus meant for us to be together! He was using my religious beliefs and twisting them around. I was so confused. I kept wondering if I was missing something or if he knew something that I didn't. I would go to work, trying to please him as my boss, but he was looking for being pleased in other ways.

There were times when he would ask if I could help him close up the funeral home after a visitation. He would allow me to go home and feed the boys dinner, then I would return to work. When I showed up, Matt would offer me a drink, the alcoholic kind that we both drank. He had started offering drinks while we worked long hours — up to nineteen hours at a stretch when it was busy. That month, it was busy.

It takes on average three days to do a normal funeral from start to finish. In January, we had thirteen death calls. I was at the funeral home approximately sixteen hours a day, seven days a week. When I would go back to help finish the work for the night, such as moving the flowers other necessary things, Matt would make an advance and it would get really physical.

I documented whatever I could and in my most desperate hours, I called a suicide hotline just to have someone to talk to who couldn't report names and cause me to lose my job over my boss's behavior.

In absolute desperation and on the verge of a nervous breakdown, I figured if my cold husband heard that his emotional abuse made me vulnerable to my boss's advances, then we could work on our marriage and that would give me the strength to tell Matt to leave me alone and he would know that I meant it.

So on June 11, 1995, I told John that I had let my boss's advances go too far. I reassured him that nothing was going on and said not to blame Matt, because I knew John was mean enough to kill him if he had the motive, but John would never kill me if I reassured him nothing was going on. The next day, I went to work and told Matt that my husband knew what pressure he had been putting me under and that I wanted him to stop it. I think he got the message and he backed off for a while. A few times after that he would be drinking at work and would grab me inappropriately and I would burst into tears and tell him to stop.

Though I'd told John that nothing was going on with Matt, I said if we did not work on our marriage, we would end up getting divorced and I didn't want that. I expressed my love for John and my deepest desire to have a good marriage, in the hopes that he would finally realize that it takes two to make a marriage work. We did talk a bit for a few weeks, but John refused to go for counseling.

One day, after four months of no improvement, I mentioned that maybe we needed to separate. I didn't really want to separate, I just thought if I said that, John might realize that if he refused to communicate, the marriage wasn't going to work out. I guess he didn't want to deal with his feelings, because he grabbed an overnight bag and walked out the door. That was the last week of September 1995.

I stood there and cried in shock and panic because at the time, I was taking twenty-one credits in college, was on call for work twenty-four hours a day, seven days a week, was taking care of my disabled mother, and had my two boys, ages eight and eleven. Now I was all alone!

I was in for the toughest test of my life up to this point. I only saw John in passing a few times when he would pick up the boys. He was very nasty and verbally abusive. I begged him to stop that behavior in front of the boys but to no avail. I tried to still be kind and even offered him time to come over and talk, but he refused and would curse at me.

A few weeks later, he showed up at the house and loaded up his truck with the guest room furniture and some other belongings. I guess he decided he didn't want to work things out.

It was about a week later that I first talked to a man named Richard. He was at a visitation for his friend's father and, of course, I was working it. When I opened the door to the funeral home, he said, as he kindly put his arm around me, "Darling if you weren't married, I'd ask you out on a date."

I, in my mind, almost fell over. He didn't know that I had just separated. As in all small towns, people gossip, and our town was no different. While at the visitation, Richard heard that I was separated. One week later, he came to the funeral home and asked me if I would go to the annual fish fry that would be held that weekend. It was an event that thousands go to and my boss said it would be good for me to go to for the visibility of the funeral home personnel.

I was so scared to accept the invitation. I had never dated anyone except John. I asked some of my friends that knew Richard very well and they told me he was well respected and trustworthy, so I did say yes. But I wouldn't go with him; I would meet him there and he would give me the ticket to get in.

We talked that night and got to know each other. That was the beginning. He continued calling me and I knew I had to keep our relationship a secret, so as not to aggravate John.

Still trying to help John see that we could save our marriage, I offered to make time for him to come over and discuss the situation, but it fell on deaf ears.

A few weeks later, John came over again. He seemed "all nice" and offered to help me take in the groceries, as I had just gotten back from the store. We then went out on the screen porch and he wanted to talk for the first time. We talked for about fifteen minutes and, weeks later, I found out during court proceedings that he was secretly taping our conversations to use against me to try to get custody of the boys. But before that particular conversation was over, John told me that the boys told him that they had been fishing with a guy named Richard.

"Who was this guy?" John wanted to know.

I told him that it was someone I had met just recently and he took us fishing. John then asked if I was going to date him. Being an honest person and feeling that John was the one who left me, I told him that I might consider dating. When I said that, John flew into a rage so violent that he swung around and slammed his fist into the glass sliding doors on the porch. Immediately, his hand swelled up.

I was really scared, but I was also concerned for John, as he was in pain. His truck was a stick shift and I knew he couldn't drive to the hospital, so I took him to the emergency room, where they put a cast on his hand because he had broken it. When we got back to the house, he asked me to tell his father if I saw him that John fell and broke his hand when he was packing boxes, not that he broke it punching the door in anger. His father would be very angry that his son would be that out of control.

For the next few months, John made my life miserable and frightening. I was stressed to the breaking point. He was doing everything he could to make me lose my job, including calling my boss. One night in January 1996, John even called Matt's wife, Nancy, and told her that Matt and I were having a torrid affair, which John knew we were not. It was his way of trying to get more control in this situation, and revenge.

Matt called to tell me this and in desperation, to try to calm John down, I went to where he was staying. When I arrived, he met me at the door with a handgun to try to intimidate me. I went in, anyway, and told him to please stop what he was doing, as hurting me was only hurting the boys and we should try to work out our problems civilly.

He looked me straight in the eye, with the revolver behind the cushion of the couch, and said, "If I don't like what is happening in the future with you and the boys, I will kill you."

I knew him well enough that I went the next day to the person in charge of getting me a restraining order to protect me. I wanted it on record that he was getting dangerous, but I was told that the way the law in Virginia was written, because he hadn't hit me, I didn't qualify! When Matt kept making advances, I couldn't take it anymore.

On the morning of February 16, 1996, I woke up really early; it was snowing. I poured a white Russian and wrote Matt a note, telling him I'd had enough of what he was doing. I went to the funeral home at seven o'clock, left the note, took my personal belongings, and then left my key and pager on the counter and went home.

About an hour after I got home, the phone started to ring. I wouldn't answer. Ten minutes later, I saw Matt drive up to my house, come to the front door, and leave. I went to the front door and found that he'd left my key, pager and a note. It said he didn't understand why I would leave like this and he needed an explanation.

The phone kept ringing and I wouldn't answer. Finally, downstairs, where I had another phone, my mother answered and yelled upstairs that it was Richard calling. I took the call.

Richard knew I was quitting and asked if I had done it. I said I had and asked why. He said his father had just died! I couldn't believe it.

I paused, then said, "For you, Richard, I will be there. Meet me at the funeral home to make arrangements at ten o'clock."

I realized that my desire to serve the community was stronger than my desire to get away from my boss and I needed to be strong and really make Matt understand where I stood. I got dressed and showed up at nine o'clock, just as if I were going to work on time. When I walked in, I looked right at Matt and said, "I am not here to give you an explanation for quitting; I am here to serve the Worsham family. Richard's father just died and I got the call and they want me to take care of him."

Matt was shocked. He said he didn't know if he should let me back, but he knew how important the Worsham family was in the community, so he said, "Okay. You do the whole funeral; it's all yours."

He left for the weekend and only showed up for the actual funeral service.

While I dealt with these threats to my professional life, though at the same time nearing the time I would be earning my degree and taking tests for my license that would enhance my career plan, I continued to feel the effects of my estranged husband's wrath. John seemed to devote February to sabotaging memories. One time, he came to our house and broke the glass out of all the picture frames. Soon after, he stole every picture of himself out of every album and frame. As painful as this was for me, it was completely in line with the mental and emotional abuse John favored.

Of course, I wasn't the only one to suffer during this time. Matthew and Michael received their share of the abuse, both directly and indirectly, as John's pawns in his efforts to hurt me. No matter how nice I was or how much I agreed with John, he would find something to cause trouble about. I will just list some of them.

Among other things, John took me to court, claiming that I was making the boys fat. He was the one buying them junk food and anything they wanted when he had them for his weekends. He badmouthed me to them any time he could, saying things that were untrue and hurtful. They lived with me and they lived the truth, so he was confusing them. Sadly, John refused to agree with any wish they had if I made the request. And he even took them to a child psychologist for therapy four months before the custody hearing to make himself look like a better parent. From what they told me, it made them more stressed.

The divorce court proceedings progressed. John had visitations with the boys whenever he wanted; I didn't try to keep him away from them. I was trying to make a miserable situation less miserable by agreeing to almost all terms brought up.

In April 1996, John showed up at the house and Michael begged me to ask his dad to give him his baseball glove back, as he had it in his truck. When I went over and asked him for the glove and told him that Michael was crying, John just spit in my face and called me dirty names. I turned away and went into the house. John followed me in and started to rant and rave with the most vile and dirty language and I again begged him to stop, as the boys were downstairs in the basement.

I then said I would call the police and John said, "Go ahead," and handed me the phone, as if taunting me to do it, so I did. The police came and spoke to John and asked him to leave peacefully.

At work the next few months went by normally as we put our problems behind us. Business was just business except Matt, on a few separate occasions said very controlling things about my personal life. He told me what church to start going to and also what weekends I would be "allowed" to date Richard! It was not his place to run my life. While I was an intern, he had control, but at this point my internship was over, and I was close to earning my degree. However, Matt did say that, if by chance I lost custody of my boys when the divorce was final, he would think about letting me go because I wouldn't be a good reflection on the business!

I was shocked and said so. He said he didn't think he would do that, but his attitude did affect something that was just about to happen and was important to me. The county newspaper, which was owned by Matt's best friend, David, was about to print a story about my efforts to become licensed. David had watched how much work I was doing, as we talked almost every day. He was amazed at the struggles I had to overcome to accomplish my degree and work at the same time. He wanted to publish an article about me and asked for a nice picture, which Matt took. It was during this conversation about the upcoming custody issues that Matt told me that he didn't want the article to be run in the paper. It never did get printed.

Picture taken of me at work for the newspaper article

Chapter 6

In May 1996, I graduated from college with my degree in funeral service and, having finished my internship the previous October, I earned my license as a director/embalmer in July. I had been so determined to do well that I graduated with a 4.0 grade point average, which is straight A's in all of the required classes. I received an award from Phi Theta Kappa, which is the Tau Rho chapter of the National Honor Society.

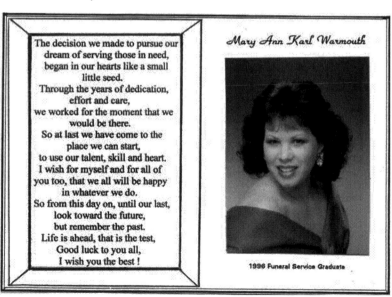

The decision we made to pursue our dream of serving those in need, began in our hearts like a small little seed.
Through the years of dedication, effort and care, we worked for the moment that we would be there.
So at last we have come to the place we can start, to use our talent, skill and heart.
I wish for myself and for all of you too, that we all will be happy in whatever we do.
So from this day on, until our last, look toward the future, but remember the past.
Life is ahead, that is the test, Good luck to you all, I wish you the best!

Mary Ann Karl Warmouth

1996 Funeral Service Graduate

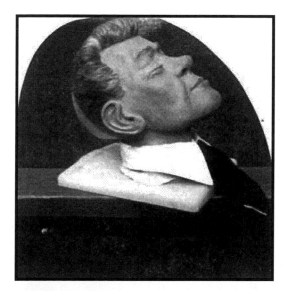

Bill Clinton's wax head.

Mr. Thornton, the head of the funeral service department on May 3, 1996.

Richard and me at graduation.

Around that time, two weeks before the final child custody hearing, Richard and I decided that we would draw up living wills. At this point, Richard had had two heart attacks and he wanted me to take care of him if anything happened to him. I also wanted him to take care of me if I had a car accident or got sick or if John did something to me. We had no idea then that I would need him for so much more, so soon.

I typed up the documents and we took them to the local bank to have them notarized. Now, even though we weren't married yet, Richard and I would be in charge of each other's legal affairs and decisions if one of us were declared mentally incompetent. We were also the beneficiaries of each other's life insurance policies, especially because I didn't want John to get anything from me.

On July 23, I went to work and, first thing in the morning, had a call from the police dispatcher about a suicide at a residence. The funeral home was requested to pick up the body and take it to the medical examiner's office in Richmond. I called Matt and we went to the house.

The gentleman who died happened to be someone I knew. He was the grandfather of the only acquaintance John had all the years we had lived in Virginia. The man had shot himself in the head because he didn't want to burden his family, due to his being in ill health. I spent the rest of the day at work, then took the boys to dentist appointments they already had set up, and then picked up the deceased gentleman from the medical examiner's office that evening.

As I was returning to the funeral home with the man's body, I passed John's apartment on the highway and saw the deceased man's grandson's vehicle parked at the apartment. The thought crossed my mind that John and this man's grandson were probably drinking alcohol to drown their troubles.

I arrived at the funeral home and proceeded to embalm the gentleman to the point that time would allow. By eleven o'clock, I finished up what could be done and called it a night and went home.

My mom was upstairs, sitting in my part of the house while I was at work so the boys wouldn't be alone. I thanked her and kissed her goodnight and she went downstairs to the in-law apartment she had in my house. I went into the boys' bedrooms, kissed them goodnight while they slept, and put on my nightgown.

Before I went to sleep, I called Richard to let him know that I was home safe from work, as he was concerned about my well being, knowing that John was a threat to me. I said goodnight to him at eleven forty-five and then fell sound asleep.

Sometime between midnight and five o'clock in the morning, John entered my home. The best that I can figure is that, under the influence of the alcohol he had been drinking with his friend, he decided that, as his friend's grandfather would no longer be a burden to his family, if I were dead, then he would not have any burdens either.

It was one week before the final custody hearing to decide whether the boys would live with John or me. He always wanted to control everything and this situation was no different. I think he figured that with me dead, everything would be solved.

I remember thinking I was dreaming about having to fend off being attacked. But it wasn't a dream; it was an actual attack.

Ultimately, I was left for dead. The worst part of it all was that the boys were the ones who found me when they woke up in the morning. They ran to a neighbor's home to call 911 because the phone lines to the house had been cut. The neighbors were girls I knew and they tried to help me before rescue arrived. I remember them asking questions, trying to get me to talk, but I could not respond.

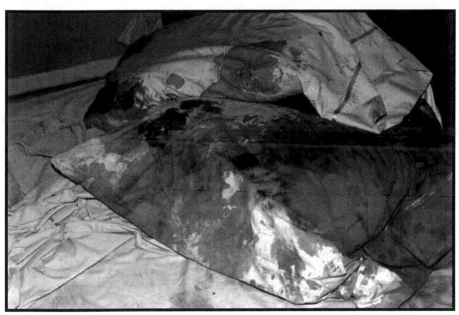

The bloody bed shows some of the blood loss.

Rescue arrived and a helicopter was called to transport me to the closest trauma center, in Richmond. When the male trauma nurse from the helicopter team tried to harness me in for the flight, my subconscious mind must have taken in his masculine voice and thought that I was still being attacked. I was in the "fight or flight" response so violently that my thrashing would have been dangerous in the helicopter, so they had to use the advanced life support vehicle to drive the forty-five minutes to the trauma center.

There, they evaluated that I had over twenty skull fractures on the right side of my skull, a broken jaw, and approximately ten stab and slash wounds to my face and head. A medical team performed six hours of brain surgery. They had to remove the part of the brain, the right temporal lobe, that had oozed out of my skull and had been too damaged to put back. They also had to remove a golf ball-sized blood clot from the center of my brain that would have killed me if left inside, and then to put pins and plates in the bone fragments, in the hopes that they would knit together in time. Facial nerves were also cut and even future reconstructive surgery would not fully rehabilitate the damage.

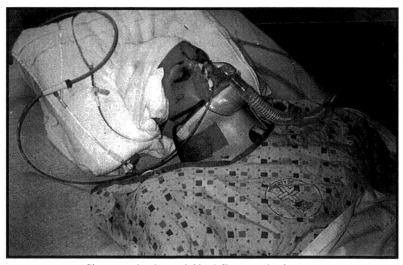

Picture my brother and friend Sheree took of me on life support four days after the attack, July 28, 1996.

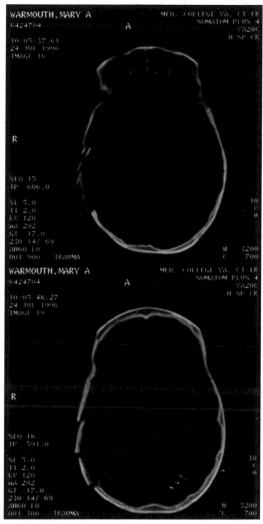

The pictures shown are called CAT scans. They are what the trauma team did to see what kind of damage was done to my skull. It shows all of the many skull fractures. The top picture is my face area; the bottom is the bottom of my head where it rests on the table when they take the scan. Like an X-ray, your bones show up white and the rest is dark. So, as you can see, the skull should be white and continuous all the way around if it is unbroken. But in my case, they found that in all levels of my head, from the top of my head to the base of my jaw (which was broken also) my skull was broken into pieces the size of corn flakes. The bone fragments were pushed into my brain and had to be plucked out during surgery. Then they pieced back what they could and held it together with titanium pins, plates and mesh to hold the brain in.

My mother called Richard's mom Jean, who then called Richard at work. Richard was the first to arrive at the hospital. His mother picked up my mom.

They told my family my chances were fifty percent or so that I might live, but if I did, there was a good chance that I would be a vegetable.

The morning of the attack, July 24, 1996, my girlfriend, Sheree Mercer, with whom I had graduated funeral school and who knew the hell I'd been going through the past year, between my estranged husband and my boss, called me at work. (This was not the Sheree who was my next-door neighbor in New Jersey.) She had moved to Florida after graduation because there was more of a market for female funeral directors in that state and she called because she wanted to see how I was doing as a newly licensed funeral director.

When Matt answered and Sheree asked to speak to me, he told her I wasn't there. He had just gotten word that I had been attacked and taken to the hospital by helicopter. She fell silent. A few months earlier, I had asked her if I were ever hurt or killed, would she be my voice from the grave, so to speak? She knew that John was the only one who was threatening to kill me and she said she would honor my request.

When Sheree heard I had been attacked, she immediately called the sheriff's office. When she told them who she was and that she was calling from Florida, they were shocked. They had just left my bedroom and done crime scene analysis. On my bedside nightstand was a piece of paper on top of my Bible. On that paper was Sheree's name, number, and address in Florida. They knew that she couldn't have known anything about the attack from where she was, so they wanted to talk to her. They immediately took her number and information and she was put on the list to be called as a witness for a trial when they had enough evidence to arrest John.

My sister-in-law, Cindy, kept a journal about this time and gave it to me the following Christmas as a keepsake, to help me know what went on for the times that I did not remember.

JULY 24, 1996 — Wednesday —

Pete (Mary Ann's brother) and I received a phone call at 10:30 pm. Pete's face was like I'd never seen before. I started asking what, who is it? He didn't answer. He started to get angry and write down some phone numbers and hung up the phone. He told me "Mary Ann has been attacked, someone smashed her head. I'm going to go down there and f'in kill whoever did this to my little sister! If it was John that bastard I'll kill him." Pete running down the stairs while I asked questions frantically. "Oh my God Pete how bad is it?" I have to go now Pete said. He got on the phone and called someone to do his work for the next day. He then called work and told them he couldn't be in until Monday. Pete continued to say he was gonna kill someone. He asked me to pack a bag for him. I didn't want him going alone. I made the suggestion that he call Sheree to come along. We searched our phone book and Pete called her. It was 11:00 pm. and one of her seven kids answered. Pete said "you have to wake her up, something has happened to Mary Ann." The child came back to the phone saying she could not wake her up. Pete hung up. Not 10 seconds passed and the phone rang. It was Sheree. Pete started saying calm down, calm down. Yes I'm going down in 20 minutes, OK Sheree was going, so I was relieved he wasn't going alone. Pete tried to call Richards Mom but some strange message came on telling him that the person he was trying to reach was not available. He called the operator. They said the phone was busy. Pete went to the car, now he had tears in his eyes. He just kept saying "how could someone do this to my baby sister." He promised me he wouldn't kill anyone and he would call in the morning. I was so upset, I just wanted to know so much. I fell asleep around 2 am.

JULY 25, 1996 — Thursday —

The phone rang at 7:20 am. Pete thank God. He told me he made it safely. He and Sheree had stayed at a hotel because they had arrived around 5:30 and they wanted to sleep a few hours. They had talked to Mom at Richard's mother's house and they were meeting to go to the hospital. Pete said John's sister Kathy had taken the boys and he did not like that. He said he would call me from the hospital.

4:40 pm. — Pete called, he said he's at the hospital and he's crying. He cannot believe how someone could have done this. It's bad, really bad. The nurse Carol is being really helpful. He says you have a drain in your head that drains fluid from your brain. He said that you were in surgery for 6 hours. The Dr.s had to put in plates and pins after they removed the right temporal lobe of your brain due to the massive damage to the tissue. You were on a respirator and monitors were in your head keeping track of the pressure inside your brain. You also had a feeding tube in your stomach, a heart monitor and a catheter to drain your urine. Pete cried and cried. He told me he was staying the night. I called your mom when I got off the phone and she told me what happened from her perspective. She was a mess. She said you came home from work at 11 pm. and you walked in to see her. You went to bed about 11:30 and you said you were going to talk to Richard before going to sleep. The next morning at 6:30 or 7 ish. Mike came down screaming "mommy is hurt, there's blood everywhere!" He was crying I don't want mommy to die. Mom tried to phone 911 but the phone line was dead. She tried her phone and it was dead also. She went upstairs and you were lying on the bed, blood was everywhere. Mom ran to the neighbors house about 50 feet away to use their phone. When she returned you were on the floor. She asked you who did this to you but you could not respond. You were admitted to the hospital at about 8 am. They wanted to fly you by helicopter but you were so combative with the flight nurse they could not do it. One of the neighbors across the road knew John's sister and called her. John's sister came and took the boys saying she had "legal" right to take them.

FRIDAY —JULY 26, 1996 —

Pete called me and told me he was going to Richards mother's house and today he was going to get the boys. He told me that when he was talking to you, you squeezed his hand. He was so happy. He said every time the medication was lightened up you would start moving around and when asked you would squeeze their hand or move your fingers. We all wanted to know how the investigation was going but the police would not say too much. The detectives Vernon Poe and Greg Neal came to see your mom and told her they did not want John's family to have the boys. This made us feel better. John was the # 1 suspect. Pete, mom, Sheree and Richard went to the house. Your bedroom door was shut with a small square of police crime scene tape across your bedroom door that said "do not enter — crime scene." John's father was bringing the boys for a visit, to see their Uncle Pete and Sheree. What his father did not know was Richard had gone to court, because you had given Richard legal power of attorney, and he had gotten temporary custody of the boys. This was until Wednesday's custody hearing. Mr. Warmouth was upset. He said, "Your opening a whole new can of worms." But of course the police knew what they were doing. Pete had talked with the boys about what had happened. He said mommys hurt and right now we just want her to get better. The boys really wanted to go to the hospital and see you but the doctors wanted to wait a few days. We were all nervous about them seeing you hooked up to all the wires and machines.

Later that night your mom called me and told me that Pete was being silly about something. I asked what. She said Pete started to wonder about Richard. She said Pete thinks Richard may have been involved in this. Your mom reassured me by telling me that she knew how nice Richard had been to you and to her for months, taking care of the boys and things around the house while you were going to college and all and that you had written a living will and the morning of the attack she had called Richard's mom who called him at work. He left work immediately and went straight to the hospital to be there for you and find out who had done this terrible thing. The detectives knew Richard very well as he is known in the county being a lifelong resident and they knew he was trustworthy. But Pete did not know Richard and he was just uneasy about the whole terrible situation.

JULY 27, 1996 —

Pete called from the hospital again and he was very upset. He said you kept twitching and it was upsetting to watch. The nurses were trying to lower your pain medication. Pete told me that Sheree's husband Dave would come to pick her up on Friday because that was the only time he could come and get her. I then talked to your mom and we went over all the events of the past year. I recalled when speaking to her she told me she never told the police about the death threats John had made. Was this a crime of passion. We figured it wasn't a stranger because it was done so quietly. The dog never barked, the person came and left and the boys and mom were not woken up and the person had to have a key to get in the house. The person knew where the phone lines were and they knew mom was down stairs. There are just too many things pointing to John or Richard. But John was the only one packed with motive. We all know he was packed full of it and how much of an angry person he had been thru the years. But how could someone who had been kind and funny and nice during those years also do something this horrifying to someone. But that is where the saying a crime of passion comes from.

JULY 28, 1996 —

Pete went to the train station to pick up your Aunt Jeanne who was coming from Florida. She said she was going to stay for 3 weeks to help your mom. Pete said something strange was going on. John's sister Kathy kept calling and asking when she could come and clean the bedroom up. Everyone thought that was strange, she had no other interest in helping any other way. That reminds me, Sheree wanted to take a shower and needed shampoo. When she went into your master bathroom she was shocked by the amount of blood everywhere, including the toilet bowl. You must have thrown up and there was bloody handprints on the walls. Pete also said that while at the house he thought about the person who did this leaving the scene. WHICH WAY WOULD THEY HAVE LEFT THE HOUSE ? HE PROCEEDED TO WALK FROM THE FRONT DOOR TO THE ROAD DIAGONALLY AND HE FOUND A BRAND NEW SCREWDRIVER LAYING ON THE GRASS !!. He called the police immediately. When they arrived he showed it to them. They took pictures of it and took it away. IT HAD THE NAME OF THE COMPANY JOHN WORKED FOR ON IT. At the hospital Pete came to say goodbye even though he did not want to leave but he had to get back to work or he would lose his job. Pete sat alone with you and kept telling you how much he loved you. You opened your eyes and looked at him. Then you picked up your hand and made the "I LOVE YOU GESTURE" with your fingers. He was overjoyed! I could hear it in his voice.

Pete and I had discussed earlier about taking some pictures of you. We know you would want them so we did. We will give them to you when you are ready. We are all so worried about you. There will be good days and bad but we are so proud of you so far.

JULY 29, 1996 —

You spoke for the first time today. Coming out of a coma is hard work. We are so happy. The nurses asked if you wanted TV and you said yes. Brain fluid is leaking out of your right ear and from your head where one of the screws was. You will be moved out of ICU today. Great news. I am coming to Virginia at the end of August and I can't wait! We are all looking forward to it. I wish I could call you but there is a strict code to get a hold of you. You are under an alias for your protection. This was done by the police. Your name is Doris Toor. And then you have to have a code name of Garfield to tell them when they ask. All of this had to be done even for anyone to see you in the hospital. Richard was the only one who knew it and he got everyone in to see you including your mom, Pete, Sheree and Aunt Jeanne and Richard's mom Jean. Richard also went to the hospital every morning before he went to work to see how you were doing. I think he really loves you so I am more at ease about him.

JULY 30, 1996 —

The emergency custody hearing was today, and what I heard was that John's parents were fighting tooth and nail for custody of the boys saying that you and your mom were not able to take care of them. The children were appointed a lawyer of their own by the court. John has visitation rights until the next hearing on September 3rd. Sheree and I decide to give John a call. We were curious about how he felt about what was going on. Sheree talked to him. He was very angry as usual. He says he is being violated by the police, they came and took all his knives, guns and went through all his stuff. Sheree says "but how do you feel about Mary Ann, aren't you concerned about her at all?" He said they won't tell me a f'in thing. He seems more worried about custody. Sheree said she felt like she was talking to a sicko.

AUGUST 1, 1996 —
In court Wednesday the judge told John he could pick up the boys and only drive into the driveway and honk the horn. Do not enter the house. Of course he came unannounced and did not follow the rules. He just walked into the house, scaring your mom out of her wits. He acted like his shit did not stink. He picked up a newspaper article about you and the attack and started to read it. Your mother told him he was not to come inside just beep. He argued with her. As soon as he left your mom called the lawyer and told him John was not doing what the judge ordered. What nerve. I think John is really pushing things.

AUGUST 3, 1996 —
I was told that the detective Vernon Poe came to talk to you today and see if you remembered what happened to you. I can't wait to hear what goes on and I can't wait to visit you. I could not come today as expected but I will be there the first week in September for your first face to face custody battle with John. I love you.

God Bless Cindy Karl for keeping this journal for me.

My memories of that time were a lot of pain and sleep. The first things I recall were the nurses talking around me. The most vivid thing I remember, as far as feelings and emotions, occurred the day after the attack and surgery that saved my life. Richard came and sat next to my bed. He put my hand on his face. I felt his beard and all of a sudden, a feeling of calm and peace came over me. I knew deep inside that I was safe. I knew he was there; I knew it was him even though I didn't see him and in my head, that meant everything was okay, even though at the time, I didn't even know I was in the hospital.

What I vividly remember from my time in intensive care is that I could hear the voices of people whom I knew very well — my brother, mother, aunt, Sheree (my good friend from New Jersey), and various others. Some of the comments were well intended, but I could also hear the doctors removing some of these people when they said things.

When I was able to understand conversations better, I once heard the doctor who was monitoring my brain functions for epileptic episodes make a comment to my mother that I might have a seizure. She said, "Oh no, who is going to drive me to my doctor's visits?" The doctor said, "Don't say those things; she can hear you!" I did hear that comment and a lot of other ones. My mother was more concerned at times about who was going to keep taking care of her, not if I would survive.

When I came out of the coma, I felt an incredibly excruciating pain in my head. I had never before felt pain that intense and I didn't know what or why I was in the hospital. All the nurses would say to me is, "You had an accident." This is what's done with head injured people for their own protection. I was finally moved into my own room and I received physical therapy and it was hard work. I had to do it at least once a day to practice getting my balance back. Since my the bones on the right side of my head had been crushed, including all the small bones in my right ear, I had lost a lot of my ability to keep my balance. I had also lost my senses of taste and smell, which is common with a severe brain injury, and so had no interest in eating.

At one point in my recovery, I became conscious of a tube coming out of my nose. I asked what it was and they said a feeding tube. Since in my mind I was a healthy person, I just reached up and pulled on it until it came out. The same thing happened with the IV in my arm. After that, they strapped my arms down to the sides of the bed to keep me from removing necessary medical things that kept me alive.

I do remember a funny incident after I woke up, where the nurse came into the room to check my brain function and my Aunt Jeanne and Richard's mother, Jean, were in the room. The nurse asked, "Who are these two people?" I answered, "Jean and Jeanne."

The nurse looked at them and back at me and shook her head. She said, "No, honey, that can't be. Think hard and tell me again." Just then both Jeanne and Jean told the nurse, "She is right, we are both named Jean!" So the nurse wrote down in her chart that my mind was working quite well. Ha, ha.

I remember the day they asked me if I wanted to look in a mirror and I said, "Sure." I saw the stab wounds to my face for the first time, but I wasn't really too upset. I figured they would heal and joked that I could just go to the funeral home and use the wax there to fill in the holes and I would look just fine.

It wasn't until Detective Poe sat next to my bedside that I was aware of why I was in the hospital. I knew Vernon from my job and I just thought he was visiting me. He asked me if I knew anything about why I was there and when I couldn't come up with anything, he told me I had been attacked. I didn't get upset and we just talked. With some embarrassment, I told him the only person who would do such a thing was John. He had told me he would kill me six months earlier.

I was discharged after only twenty-two days, to the amazement of the doctors and others involved in my care, but I wasn't allowed to go back to my house to live because it was the scene of the crime. Also, before I was attacked, I had agreed to turn over the house to John as part of the divorce agreement. Finally, the police simply didn't want my whereabouts known. I stayed with Jean for the first month and she cared for me while I healed from my injuries. I slept a lot for the first few weeks after my discharge, which is normal for someone with a severe head injury.

However, I desperately wanted to get back to what I was doing, which was working and taking care of my boys. I was also determined to change the Virginia laws regarding restraining orders. I eventually co-founded a taskforce and support group for the surrounding counties to help others at a time of crisis in their lives. I give more details about this later in the book, when I talk about finding one's purpose in life.

During my hospital stay, Matt sent my paycheck, which included my pay increase for earning my license. When I was discharged from the hospital, I was eager to return to my job, as I had worked so hard to get my license.

I called Matt and arranged to meet him at the funeral home a week later. When I arrived there, his car and his wife's car were there. We went into the office and he genuinely seemed happy to see me. I told him I could start work the following week, with limits only on lifting heavy things, such as bodies and caskets, for about six weeks.

Matt cast his eyes downward. He said that after I was attacked, he figured that what had happened between us physically during my internship would come out somehow and he'd better tell his wife. When he told her his version of it, she gave him the ultimatum, "either she goes or I go," meaning he had to fire me or lose his wife. Next, he said that because I was hurt so badly, I was no longer one hundred percent perfect, so we should just tell everyone that was the reason I was fired.

I broke into tears and sat there in disbelief. I felt to be terminated at the lowest point in my life, after all my effort to get my license, fend off his inappropriate behavior, and get to the point where we were back to just business, was the worst thing that could possibly happen. Not only was it illegal, I was not in any shape to get into a legal battle with him.

Soon after, the head of the funeral service department where I'd received my degree, Franklin Thornton, Jr., asked if I would be interested in being his replacement because he was retiring. We had the same education and he knew how well I had done in school and that I still wanted to work in the funeral field. I desperately wanted to take the job, but after seeing all that he had to do, I knew I wouldn't be able to handle all the details involved in running a college funeral program. I thanked him and wished him well.

If having a brain injury and being fired from a job I loved weren't enough, the following months were a living hell because John was walking around free, as if nothing had happened. He tried to have our two sons with him as much as possible, even though Richard had gone to the county courthouse right after I was attacked and filed an emergency petition that granted my disabled mother custody of my sons. This way I was allowed to have them because she lived with me. All because of the living wills I had written two weeks prior to my attack.

When I was well enough to go to court in September, two months after the attack, I was given custody of the boys. This was a loss for John, of course, and in his typically hurtful way, he told the boys that actually they had lost, because now they were with me.

When I had stepped out of the car that day, with my brother, Pete, and sister-in-law, Cindy, by my side, I saw John in the distance. I'd been very nervous, but as we got closer, I noticed a lot of police milling around because John was the number one suspect and the police were afraid of what might happen when we confronted each other. When I was closer, I saw John's parents and sister and as I passed John, he turned his head and refused to look at me. It was as if he were ashamed to see what he had done.

Richard wanted my boys, my mother, and me to have our own place to live, so he lent us his home and he moved in with his mother, who lived next door. Not surprisingly, John found a way to use this arrangement as an opportunity for control and abuse. A few months after we moved into Richard's house and about a month after the divorce was final, but before Richard and I were married, John made a deal with the boys that if Richard spent the night with me and they told him, they would get a dollar!

Throughout the months that we worked toward finalizing the divorce, John continued the spiteful and abusive behavior he had subjected the boys and me to for years. Once, he played a fake tape recording for Matthew and Michael that was supposed to be Richard's ex-wife saying that she and her son had been beaten. And one night, when Michael was wearing pajamas with bulls on them, John told him, "If you mess with the bull, you get the horns. Your mother deserved those." He took even random comments and turned them into chances to say something hateful about me. When Matthew was over at John's house one weekend, he asked John to "call Mom and tell her we will be late." John replied, "I could call her quite a few things."

Chapter 7

It took the police a long time to gather all the evidence they wanted in the case to make sure it would be done right at the trial. They didn't want another O. J. Simpson-type investigation mess and a "not guilty" verdict.

To make sure my divorce would be final as soon as possible, I had to agree to everything and not delay the process. For instance, John wanted both of the vacuums we had owned. I didn't understand, except that his parents had bought us one as a gift and we bought one together with what is called marital money. We should have each kept one in the divorce, but to argue over it would have caused a delay, so I just let them both go. He also wanted the Christmas tree. I figured I could get another one, so I let it go, too.

At one point during this time, John's father had the nerve to tell me that he thought I was just trying to get his son in trouble. He said I must have caused my own injuries and was just blaming them on his son!

When all things were settled, the divorce became final on December 5, 1996. I had become one of those things my mother had warned me against — divorced. With all that was going on, I no longer worried if it made me "bad," as I'd thought in my youth that it would.

Mary Ann Worsham

Estranged husband indicted for assault

by Patience Branum
Staff Writer

The Powhatan County grand jury last week issued a true bill indicting John Joseph Warmouth for the assault of Mary Ann Warmouth earlier this year. He has been charged with aggravated malicious wounding, and if convicted, could receive a punishment of 20 years to life in prison.

The investigation by the sheriff's office took approximately five months to complete. "It was a combination of physical evidence, interviews and crime scene work," Undersheriff Greg Neal stated. "We sent several bags [of materials from the crime scene] to the state forensics lab."

The attack with which Warmouth has been charged took place some time during the night of July 24, 1996, while Ms. Warmouth was sleeping in a bedroom of her house on Daphne Lane. The attacker beat the victim about the head and stabbed her several times in the face. She was found in the morning by members of her family.

"This was classified by experts as a 'personal attack,'" Neal explained. "There was nothing to indicate robbery was a motive, [for instance. It had] one purpose—to harm her."

The brutal attack created great tension throughout Powhatan, coming just ten days after two teenagers were murdered about two miles away from the Warmouth home.

The Warmouths had been separated for some time at the time of the assault. The sheriff's office had been called to the house on previous occasions, both before and after their separation. They are now divorced.

Warmouth turned himself in to the sheriff's office after the grand jury issued the direct indictment. He was released after a family member put up the $25,000 secured bond set by the court.

A trial date was scheduled to be set Tuesday, December 17, but Warmouth's attorney, Michael Morchower, asked for a continuance. It was granted, and a trial date will not be set until February.

December 1996—Newspaper story about estranged husband's indictment for the first count of just aggravated malicious wounding. He was not indicted with the second charge of statutory burglary by the grand jury until February of 1997. He still walked free.
"Estranged Husband Indicted for Assault," Richmond Times-Dispatch, December 2, 1996.

72

of only about $25,000, and he walked right out the next day. Now he was even angrier than before and I was more fearful. The police kept surveillance on the road Richard's house was on, knowing how dangerous John was, and the 911 dispatcher knew if any calls came from that address, the police would be on alert.

Richard asked me to marry him on Christmas Eve and we were married on February 1, 1997. Now, instead of being a member of the traditional family of my dreams — which had become a nightmare, anyway — I was a member of a "blended" family.

What bonded us together so quickly and has continued to be the glue that holds us together is that we share a lot of experiences that most couples don't. The biggest one is that we were both married for fourteen years and both of our ex-spouses went to prison for the terrible things they did to us. Richard's second wife forged his name on thirty-seven credit cards and on a bank note to refinance the house, then took all the money and left him penniless. Fourteen years of hard work all gone, in that case. His ex-wife only spent three months in jail.

While we still have disagreements and problems as any two people will have, we took vows for better or worse and we know how bad "worse" can really be. We just know we have to trust each other. That's the biggest part of our success, but also the desire to enjoy life and not fight. If we do, we work on a compromise, not "who is right."

It was good that our marriage was strong from the beginning because, though we'd already been through a lot together, there was much more to come. In the months after we wed, we slept with a baby monitor on the nightstand and at the back door to listen for strange sounds. We feared seeing John every time he came to pick up the boys, at the Little League games I had signed Michael up for, etc.

One big stress factor in remarriage is the "Brady Bunch" issue — whose kids are whose and how to treat them fairly. I have been very lucky in that Richard has treated my sons

like they were his own. This has been an even bigger blessing than it would normally be, considering how Matthew
and Michael's biological father has treated them.

I had to speak to the State of Virginia's prosecutor many
times that spring to prepare for the trial. We went over all
the evidence. It was mostly circumstantial. I went for a hypnosis session ten weeks after I was released from the hospital to try to help me remember details of the night of the
attack. Hypnosis is not some TV show magic; it's just a way
that someone who is experienced in it talks to you when
you are relaxed, which may help you remember things you
consciously try to block out. I was asleep when the attack
started and since I was brain injured so badly, my memory
was in only bits of the event itself, such as knowing it was
John by the sounds, such as grunts, that he made as we
struggled, and the word that he uttered — "paybacks!"

I clearly remembered that when I sensed I was alone in
the room again, I struggled off the bed. I was feeling sick
to my stomach and headed to the bathroom to throw up in
the toilet. Stopping at the front window to look out, I saw
John's car driving down the road, away from our home.
They verified that my bloody handprint was dusted off that
front window.

Due to the way criminal law is written, statements giv-
en under hypnosis are not admissible in court. Because of
the delay between the event and my memory of it, it was
said that I was making it (the memory) up. Actually, the
condition is known as repressed memory and was a result
of the severe trauma I suffered. The bottom line was that
what I remembered didn't count and I would be made to
sit through the trial as though I were dead, like other well-
known and unfortunate victims, such as Laci Peterson, Nicole Brown Simpson and Lori Hacking. The difference was
that I was suffering terribly.

Consequently, my testimony was limited to events that
happened leading up to the attack, such as when John said
that he would kill me if he didn't like what was going to

happen in the future with the boys, his verbal abuse, and threatening behavior. Remember, the attack occurred one week before the final custody hearing.

As the trial date neared, John continued to try to make me look like the bad guy. A week before the first criminal trial, he told the boys, "You will see who is lying; it will prove your mother has been." John and his parents kept telling Matthew and Michael that John didn't do it.

The prosecution's case was based on the following points and testimony: A forensic expert on handprint analysis confirmed that, of the bloody handprints left on my sheets, seventeen lines and measurements matched John's fingers and hands. Just as importantly, there were no lines, marks or measurements that didn't match. My attacker had cut the one phone line out of six, which disabled both my mother's separate phone line and the house phone. A phone company expert related how only someone who knew exactly which wire to cut could disable the phone system the way it had been done. This was important because John had wired the house for the phones. John also knew the quietest way to get into the house and the house layout, plus he had keys to get in.

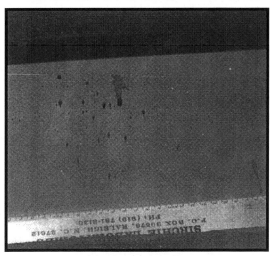

Splatter measurements.

75

The phone wire that was cut.

My bloody handprint on the window.

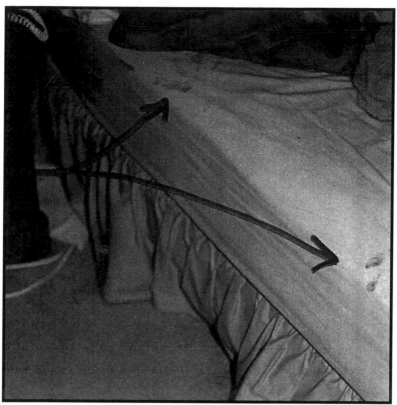

John's bloody handprints on the bed.

We also had testimony from people who knew John and about his cold, sarcastic character, as well as about his mistreatment of the boys and, especially, of me. Additionally, my brain surgeon discussed that it appeared a hammer and knife were what was used to inflict the injuries.

The lead detective in the case testified that when he met John at work the morning the police found me, he told John that I was alive and would probably be giving a statement soon. I was in a coma, of course, but John was not only shocked that I was alive (because he left me for dead), but that I would be talking. The detective said John's immediate reaction was a sudden dropping of his eyes (loss of

Mary Ann Worsham

Richmond Times-Dispatch

Assault leads to conviction

Victim's ex-husband to be sentenced in October

BY CHARLES BOOTHE
TIMES-DISPATCH STAFF WRITER

Nearly a year after it started, a case that some Powhatan residents called the county's version of the O.J. Simpson saga is over.

The case ended Wednesday when John Joseph Warmouth was convicted in Powhatan Circuit Court of statutory burglary and aggravated and malicious wounding in an attack on his estranged ex-wife.

A jury of nine men and three women deliberated about three hours. They had listened to two days of testimony that included tales of infidelity, deception, planted evidence and an estranged husband full of rage.

Almost 30 witnesses were called during the trial, among them a forensic scientist, an "impression" expert and a handwriting analyst.

And before the trial got under way, Warmouth's now ex-wife filed a $1 million civil suit against him, claiming he inflicted permanent physical damage in the bloody attack.

Others asleep nearby

Sometime during the night of July 23, 1996, Mary Ann Warmouth Worsham, 37, was attacked by an intruder while she slept. Her two children were sleeping in a nearby bedroom and her mother was asleep downstairs in her Daphne Lane home.

She doesn't remember what happened, but she was found the next morning lying unconscious beside her blood-splattered bed.

She was hospitalized for several weeks as a result of blows to the head. Her face and body had been slashed and stabbed, leaving her badly scarred. She also had hearing loss and partial facial paralysis.

In their investigation, police found no weapons at Worsham's home, though the telephone lines into the house had been cut. There was no sign of forced entry into her home and nothing had been taken.

Police quickly turned their attention to Warmouth, 38, from whom Worsham had been separated for eight months. But a search of his house and car produced no evidence, and there were no other suspects.

After Worsham was released from the hospital, she eventually decided to move. During the move, a dispatch from Warmouth's former employer was found under Worsham's bed. She turned it over to the police on Nov. 1.

On Dec. 11, a grand jury returned an indictment against Warmouth for statutory burglary and aggravated malicious wounding, charges that carry the possibility of life in prison.

Powhatan Commonwealth's Attorney John Lewis was confronted with building a case using primarily circumstantial evidence, with the exception of the document found under Worsham's bed months after the attack. The document had fingerprints that matched Warmouth's, Sylvia Buffington, a state forensic scientist, testified.

Warmouth's lawyer, Michael Morchower of Richmond, maintained that the document was planted by Worsham. He called a Virginia Beach handwriting analyst who testified that a date, July 18, and a time that was scribbled on the front of the document was likely the writing of Worsham.

The only other physical evidence linking Warmouth to the crime was an "impression" of part of a palm found on one of the bloody bedcovers. An expert witness on impressions, Robert Hallet, said the match with Warmouth was likely.

With no eyewitnesses and limited physical evidence, as well as no documented history of physical abuse in the relationship, Lewis tried to convince the jury Warmouth was the only one with a motive.

Lewis said Warmouth was upset about the impending divorce, about an affair his wife had had, about possibly losing custody of his children, and about being told by his wife that she was planning to remarry.

Worsham, who remarried in February, had been granted temporary custody of their sons. A hearing for permanent custody was set for July 31.

She testified at the trial that Warmouth had threatened her and had at one point put his fist through a sliding glass door in anger, breaking a bone in his hand.

No threats made

Morchower said the glass incident did happen, but he said no threats had been made. Warmouth did not testify.

The defense called several witnesses to show that Warmouth was not violent and was good to his children. One witness was Joseph Higgins, Warmouth's brother-in-law, who was a deputy chief of the Richmond police force and is now an investigator for the law firm of Morchower, Luxton and Whaley.

Higgins said he talked with Worsham on Aug. 25, 1995, and first learned of their marital difficulties. Worsham, he said, told him Warmouth was "not socially acceptable to her friends" and that she wanted to be somebody important in Powhatan County.

Higgins also said Worsham was not cooperative with visitations after the couple separated.

Lewis insisted, though, that Warmouth was the only one with a motive and had easy access to the house.

Lewis said Warmouth used a key to the house that he still had. He also knew exactly which telephone line to cut to disable all lines coming into the house because he wired them, Lewis said.

In a bizarre twist to the story, Lewis said Warmouth tried to create a diversion less than two weeks after the assault.

Wendy Hodges testified that, at 10:30 p.m. on Aug. 5, a man knocked on her front door. Hodges and her daughter were in the front room while her husband slept. She said her husband's car was parked behind the house, out of view. She looked through the "peephole" on the front door, saw a man, then awakened her husband.

Her husband, Joe Hodges, testified that he opened the door and talked briefly to the man who said that his car was "broke" on nearby George's Road and he needed a "jump" to get it started. But after Hodges put on his shoes and returned to the porch, the man was gone. The next day, they discovered their phone line had been cut.

Joe and Wendy Hodges later identified Warmouth as the man who came to their door asking for help, although Wendy Hodges could not be "100 percent sure."

Lewis said Warmouth was trying to divert attention from himself and create another suspect, but fled because he was surprised when Joe Hodges came to the door.

Incidents called unrelated

Warmouth's father, John Joseph Warmouth Sr., said he was with his son on that night. Morchower said the Hodgeses, who identified Warmouth from a sheet of six photos in January, could have been mistaken. Morchower said the two incidents were unrelated.

On the morning after the attack, Warmouth had only been told that his wife had been injured. But Powhatan Detective Vernon Poe said when he told Warmouth that his wife was still alive and was expected to give a statement, Warmouth's eyes dropped and "he began shaking and breathing shallow."

"Yes, John Warmouth is a suspect," Morchower said. "It is possible the defendant committed these crimes ... but this case has a lot of possibles and a ton of maybes ... suspicion is not sufficient."

But the jurors recommended that Warmouth be sentenced to the minimum 20 years on each of the two counts.

Circuit Judge Thomas V. Warren ordered a presentencing report and will set a sentencing date in October to decide if the two 20-year terms will be served concurrently. Warmouth will be required by state law to serve at least 85 percent of the sentence, barring any successful appeals.

Warren also denied a motion to allow Warmouth to remain free on bond until the sentencing.

Charles Boothe, "Assault Leads to Conviction," Richmond Times-Dispatch, July 9, 1997.

Assault nets 40-year term

Estranged wife was attacked with hammer and knife

A Powhatan County man convicted of a near-deadly hammer and knife assault on his estranged wife was sentenced yesterday to 40 years in prison.

John Warmouth, 38, was sentenced to 20 years for the aggravated malicious wounding of Mary Ann Warmouth Worsham as she slept in her Daphne Lane home the night of July 23, 1996. Warmouth also received 20 years for breaking and entering with a deadly weapon with intent to commit murder, said John L. Lewis III, Powhatan's commonwealth's attorney.

Judge Thomas V. Warren of Powhatan Circuit Court imposed the sentences to run consecutively.

Lewis said Warmouth probably would serve at least 32 years.

"Warmouth will be close to 80 years old before mandatory release, but he could be eligible at age 60" on a geriatric release, Lewis said.

Warmouth was convicted by a jury in July, based largely on circumstantial evidence and Warmouth's status as the only known person with a motive to hurt his then-estranged wife. At the time of the assault, witnesses said Warmouth was upset about his impending divorce, the possibility of losing custody of his children, Worsham's relationship with another man and her plans to remarry.

Worsham did remarry and carries scars from the night her head was pounded with a hammer — her skull was cracked — and her face and body were stabbed and sliced.

"Assault Nets 40-Year Term," *Richmond Times-Dispatch*, December 1997

79

eye contact usually means guilt) and then sudden, shallow breathing, which a person does when frightened.

The prosecution also told how, ten days after I was attacked, just two miles away from my home, a woman answered her door late at night when her husband was supposed to be at work. She faced a man claiming that his car had broken down and he needed to use her phone. A moment later, her husband came to the door and said he would get his shoes on and help the man, but when the husband went out the front door, the man had left.

The husband searched the road and found no broken-down car. In fear, due to the recent attack on me in the local area, the man tried to report the incident to the police, but found his phone lines had been cut! The police took mug shots of eight different men to the couple, who looked them over. Both the husband and the wife picked out John as the man at the door!

The prosecution contended that my estranged husband was trying to create a "stranger" lurking in the area to throw off the police from thinking he was a suspect. Remember, my sister-in-law Cindy wrote that John read the newspaper article that told residents to keep an eye out for any strangers in the area and I think that gave him the idea to create a "stranger."

Last, but not least, was the fact that John had the motive to kill me. He wanted control over the marital situation and the children and he was drinking the evening of the attack. The man he was drinking with had left him at ten thirty that night, so John was alone and had no alibi for the time period following that.

John's family hired the most well known defense attorney in Richmond, Virginia, with a reputation for defending the worst of the worst. If you were guilty, you should hire this guy, so to speak — similar to Mark Geragos, the lawyer who defended Scott Peterson when he was on trial for the murder of his pregnant wife, Laci. John's sister's husband was past vice-chief of police in the city and he knew whom to call when someone was in real trouble. He happened to have retired from the police force and in 1996, was working for this man as a detective.

John's lawyer presented the case and this is about all the defense could come up with: John had character witnesses saying he was a hard worker and a nice guy. It was said that John would never do something like this and have his kids find me. The defense attorney claimed that Matt's wife was the one who committed the crime or it was some stranger who came into the house. The defense also had a handprint expert of their own, who said that handprints left on a sheet are not conclusive, as is a fingerprint left on a smooth surface. That was the only rebuttal witness that they had to try to confuse the jury.

The jury received instructions on sentencing and then went to deliberate the case. They came back in three hours with the verdict — guilty on both charges. Each charge carried a penalty of twenty years to life in prison, for a total of forty years to life. The jury gave John the minimum of forty years.

John was sent to prison on July 9, 1997, but immediately filed an appeal. The appeal was heard in appellate court in spring 2000 and John was granted a new trial.

The basis of the new trial was that the testimony of the husband and wife, who identified John as the man who appeared at their home then disappeared, should not have been allowed into the trial. Sometime between 1997 and 2000, the prosecutor who had handled the first trial retired. Since the Commonwealth (State) of Virginia had a new prosecutor, I had to go over all the evidence again and prepare for all of the questions and cross-examination I would have to go through. It was going to be hell.

One thing that's important to remember is that the world didn't stop so that I could deal with the fact that my estranged husband had attacked me and left me for dead;

so that I could recover from my injuries; so that I could rebound from losing a job I'd worked so hard to earn; or so that I could make it through two criminal trials and one civil trial. My life continued and so did the lives of those around me. Their having to deal with the extraordinary events in my life, while continuing to live their normal ones, and I having to deal with their everyday concerns while trying to make sense of my exceptional ones, was stressful for everyone.

Even just the multiple head injuries would have been enough of a strain. Of course, I was in the hospital for the early stages of my recovery from the physical symptoms of my injuries, such as coma, impaired swallowing, difficulty with speech, loss of coordination in limbs (often spastic), and unstable blood pressure, heart rate, and breathing. But effects that don't show up until later and can last indefinitely include emotional symptoms, personality changes, memory loss, fatigue, and post-traumatic stress disorder (PTSD).

One area that I can certainly address is post-traumatic stress disorder. Living through the California earthquake in 1971, in which over sixty people died, has made me very sensitive to any minor earth movements. If I feel the earth move, which usually has to register over a three on the Richter Scale, I know exactly what it is.

But in reality, when I refer to my post-traumatic stress disorder, it is in reference to my attack. My family knows since then that they should *not* stand over me when I am asleep and try to wake me up. If they do, I am so startled that it will send me into an immediate panic, due to my subconscious mind going into the "fight or flight" mode. This is what the human mind will naturally do to protect itself and it's what mine does, due to how I was attacked. Also, they try not to startle me or surprise me for fun, as I startle easily. While that may be funny for others, it isn't good for me.

Other than that, I don't have too many other effects

from this disorder. I take two drugs. One (Zoloft) that I take daily is mainly for my brain injury, but it also covers the general anxiety from PTSD. The other (Xanax) is only used when I know I will face a stressful event that will trigger my PTSD, such as when I had to sit six feet away from John during the civil trial. Many soldiers returning from Iraq suffer from this disorder. For more information on PTSD and for helpful resources, please see the Resource Guide and Information.

I had to have five surgeries to repair damage that was not fixed in the first emergency surgery. During the attack, my facial nerves were cut so that my right eyebrow is paralyzed and droops. One of the stab wounds was to my cheek and now I can't smile without causing my right eye to close. It feels like when your grandma pinches your cheek. I am a happy person and smile a lot, so it is a constant reminder.

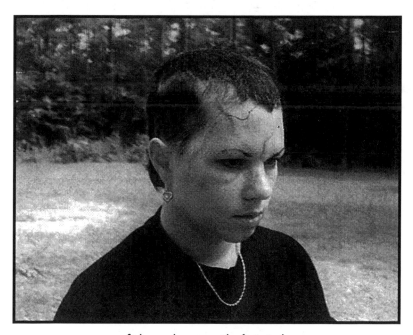

Stab wounds one month after attack.

The first year after my injury, I had to use Scotch tape to hold up my right eyebrow to keep it from making my eye close, putting it on every morning when I was putting on my makeup. I said to myself, "I need/want to get this permanently fixed," so I called a head and neck reconstructive plastic surgeon. The bones on the right side of my head in the temple area were also sinking in, so I had to have the area filled in. I could have more done, but I never had any of the work done for "getting prettier," so to speak; it was for reconstructing what was damaged so it would function better. In 1999, I had to have two vertebrae in my neck fused together. This was due to bone growth from contusions, where the hammer used in the attack hit the bone and bruised it. This bone growth pinched a nerve in my neck, causing extreme pain in my right arm and hand.

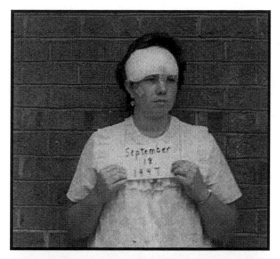

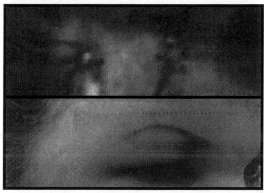

Close-up of two screws in my head.

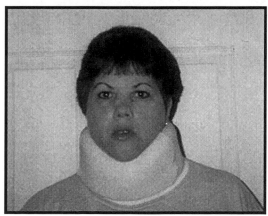

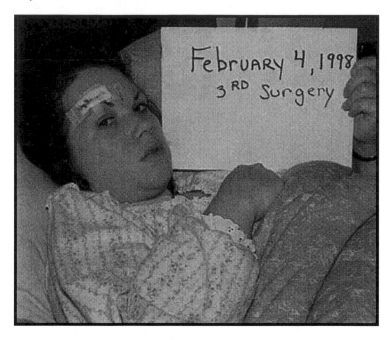

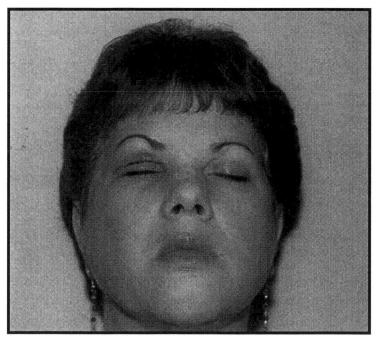

Wounding, burglary convictions reversed

BY ALAN COOPER
TIMES-DISPATCH STAFF WRITER

The Virginia Court of Appeals reversed yesterday the aggravated malicious wounding and burglary convictions of a Powhatan County man accused of attacking his estranged wife while she slept.

John Joseph Warmouth, 39, was sentenced in December 1997 to 40 years in prison for the two offenses.

His former wife, Mary Ann Worsham, was attacked with a hammer and a knife in her bedroom on Daphne Lane in April 1996. She was left comatose and remembers nothing about the incident.

Powhatan Commonwealth's Attorney John L. Lewis III contended during Warmouth's trial that Warmouth was the only known person with a motive to hurt his then-estranged wife.

At the time of the assault, witnesses said, Warmouth was upset about his impending divorce, the possibility of losing custody of his children, Worsham's relationship with another man and her plans to remarry.

Worsham did remarry after the attack.

Circumstantial evidence that connected Warmouth to the attack included his access to the house through a key, his knowledge of where to cut the telephone wire to the bedroom, and expert testimony that a bloody hand impression could have been caused by Warmouth but not by Worsham.

That evidence was properly admitted, Judge Jere M.H. Willis wrote in his opinion for the three-judge panel of the intermediate appellate court.

But testimony about two incidents was improper, and a new trial is required, Willis said.

Worsham testified that she returned home in January 1996 to find some of her jewelry damaged, a picture of her and Warmouth smashed and jewelry that Warmouth had given her missing.

Testimony about that incident should not have been allowed because nothing connected it to Warmouth, Willis said.

In the second incident, a couple identified Warmouth as the man who had come to their home about two weeks after the attack on Worsham and asked for assistance because his car had broken down.

However, the man had disappeared by the time the couple got dressed to help him, and their telephone line had been cut. Lewis contended that the testimony showed that Warmouth had cut the line to create an incident similar to the attack on Worsham and shift suspicion from him.

Willis disagreed. The testimony had no connection to the attack on Worsham and should not have been allowed, Willis said.

Newspaper story about the successful appeal that granted him a new trial.
Alan Cooper, "Wounding, Burglary Convictions Reversed,"
Richmond Times-Dispatch, April 20, 1999.

THENEWS JOURNAL

Tuesday, Aug. 29, 2000

**Defendant found guilty of
aggravated malicious wounding
and sentenced to 20 years.
Jurors deliberated
for eight hours.**

Jury convicts Warmouth of wounding in re-trial

He will likely appeal again, says Commonwealth's Attorney

Graphic pictures shown to jury in wounding trial

By Courtnie Walton

For the second time, a Powhatan County jury convicted John Joseph Warmouth for breaking into his estranged wife's house, bludgeoning her repeatedly with a hammer and leaving her near death in the summer of 1996.

The Commonwealth was forced to prosecute Warmouth again because he successfully appealed a previous conviction on technical evidentiary grounds. In the first trial, the jury sentenced him to 20 years for aggravated malicious wounding and another 20 years for statutory burglary.

This time, the jury doled out a 20-year sentence for wounding Mary Ann Worsham (then Mary Ann Warmouth) but acquitted him on the burglary charge. The jury reached its verdict Thursday at 2 p.m., after deliberating eight hours over two days.

Even after two trials, however, Warmouth might not be done. According to Powhatan Commonwealth's Attorney Bob Beasley, Warmouth will likely contest the second conviction.

"Greg Carr [Warmouth's attorney] indicated that they were going to file a notice of appeal," Beasley said Monday. According to the state's rules of criminal procedure, Warmouth must file a notice of appeal within 30 days of his most recent conviction.

Beasley did not speculate on any possible grounds for an appeal.

Establishing a motive

Last week, it was Beasley's burden to prove beyond a reasonable doubt that Warmouth entered his estranged wife's house and maliciously stabbed her with the intent to kill her.

Although the Commonwealth was not required by law to provide a motive, Beasley spent considerable time developing one in his case against Warmouth.

According to Beasley, Worsham's testimony – along with the brutality of the crime and the seriousness of her injury – pointed to a motive of sheer hatred.

Worsham showed her stab wounds to the jury.

In graphic testimony, she said the bones in the right side of her face "were crushed to the size of cornflakes. I lost 40 percent of hearing in my right ear, have paralysis in my right eyebrow, and have brain damage, which includes permanent dizziness."

Worsham was in a coma for nine days and in the hospital for 22 days following the attack. She remembers neither the details of the incident itself nor her attacker.

Dr. Malcolm Bullock an expert witness in neurology from MCV, attended to Worsham after the attack. "In my opinion, the wounds occurred with something like a hammer," he said. "There was brain material oozing out."

Courtnie Walton, "Jury Convicts Warmouth of Wounding in Re-trial," *Amelia News Journal*, August 29, 2000.

The second trial happened in August 2000, over the course of three days. There was a big delay when the jury went to deliberate. In the first trial, it only took three hours for the jury to come to a verdict. This time, the jury went out at noon, ate lunch, and kept deliberating. By late afternoon, the foreman brought word that they were having trouble.

The defense then asked the prosecution, including me, if we would accept a plea bargain (a deal) in which John would pay me a civil settlement of $150,000 for my injuries and spend only three more years in prison.

The prosecutor and I discussed this. We both knew that the deal was unacceptable because the prison sentence would be too little for the crime John committed. Also, it would mean I would have to still deal with him over child custody issues because the boys were still underage (thirteen and fifteen).

We didn't know why the jury was having trouble coming to a verdict, but it was as though John were trying to buy his freedom and the prosecutor and I would not agree to anything that the defense was trying to offer.

By five o'clock in the afternoon, the judge came into the courtroom and announced that the day was over and the jury had not reached a verdict. Court would continue in the morning at nine o'clock, sharp. I didn't sleep much at all and we arrived the next morning, anxiously awaiting the verdict. When court was called to order, the jury came in and sat down. The foreman said they still needed more time and after two more hours, came back in. The foreman then stood to read the verdict. I was holding my mother-in-law's hand and trying to keep calm.

On the first count of statutory burglary, John was found not guilty! This was because his name was on the title to the house, we were not yet divorced, and I had been unable to get a restraining order. However, on the second count of aggravated malicious wounding, he was found guilty. I was thankful that at least he would not walk free.

Then the jury had to go and discuss how much time John would be sentenced for; he faced twenty years to life for the one charge he was found guilty of. I prayed they would impose as much as they could for John leaving me permanently damaged for life, for the emotional damage he did to the boys by causing them to find me that morning, and for the years of abuse before and since the attack.

The jury came back and gave him the minimum of twenty years. I was somewhat disappointed, but again thankful that I wouldn't have to deal with him for a few years and I could raise the boys and sleep in peace. The next court proceedings I had were in civil court. I had filed a lawsuit against John in 1997, right before the first criminal trial, for monetary damages I incurred from loss of income from my job, for physical pain and suffering and permanent physical damage, and for child support for our two sons. Finally, after five years, it came to trial in May 2001.

John was brought to court under police escort. He came from prison, but was dressed nicely in a suit. The trial only lasted three hours and the jury only deliberated for one hour. They came back and awarded me $500,000 for compensatory damage, to compensate for my physical pain and suffering, so to speak, and $800,000 in punitive damages, which was to punish John for his actions. It was a total award of $1.3 million!

But handy as the money would be, I will not see a penny of it, unless I hire a lawyer to get it.

You see, when I filed the civil suit, John's parents advised him to hide his assets, which were just the house I agreed to give him in the divorce, his truck, some tools, and his pension. John sold the house to his parents for ten dollars, so in essence, they have all the assets I could ever get. I have not gotten a penny in child support from John or from his parents because they do not want me, "the enemy," as they continue to see me, to have anything.

Chapter 8

Alcohol abuse worked its way into my everyday life in 1995, when I was thirty-four years old and working at the funeral home. It started after I'd been there two years, when Matt started to sexually harass me, making the work environment so hostile and the stress unbearable.

Matt drank at work to relieve his stress from our workload. He'd offered me some and a vicious cycle began. I drank a little during the day and night and at the worst points, I would have a shot before facing him when I went into work at nine o'clock in the morning.

I did this for the two years it took to get through my internship, school, and the separation and divorce process, all the while taking care of my two sons and disabled mother by myself, at least until I was attacked.

The next period of alcohol abuse came when the Supreme Court of Virginia granted John's appeal in 2000, based on a technicality. I was still learning to live with a brain injury and reliving the attack and participating in a new trial, as both a witness and the victim; added to the pressure of feeling responsible for the trial's successful outcome, it triggered my post-traumatic stress disorder. The stress was so intense and I couldn't do anything to get out of it.

Richard, Jean, and a few others just said, "Oh, don't make a big deal about it; the evidence will turn out in your favor." But I couldn't stop the memories from playing in my head over and over again in the months leading up to the new trial. I wanted to die. My religious beliefs were against committing suicide and the only relief I found was in the effects that alcohol brings, such as loss of inhibitions and an "I don't care" attitude.

I only drank at home or at a party, but drinking made my daily problems worse, as it frustrated and embarrassed my family. After the second trial, I started going to Alcoholics Anonymous meetings in our town, both for my own desire for help and to let my family know that I was trying not to drink. They watched me like a hawk and that was very stressful, especially at social functions, where I just wanted to be treated like a "normal" person again, which I knew I could be. I only drank when under severe stress to self-medicate, not because I "needed" (craved) a drink. This felt like I was being treated like a child and I had been through too much for them to pressure me like that. Two months later, I found out that John had appealed his second conviction! It threw me into another tailspin.

I started to drink again and when I had too much, I knew that Richard would be furious and I was afraid of what would happen. I wanted help, so in desperation, I went into the woods next to our home and called the police on myself. Lying under a tree, I waited for them to come. An officer listened to my story and he knew all about my case (all the police in town knew it) and he personally wanted to help, so he took me in the squad car to the psychiatric hospital I requested for inpatient counseling. I was there for four days and returned home, determined to let go of the grip John's repeated legal filings had on my emotions.

In 2001, when I finally went through the civil lawsuit I had filed against John, it didn't bother me at all. Seeing him sitting right across the lawyer's table from me, and even testifying at the trial, didn't make me start drinking again.

I haven't had but three, maybe four, drinks in the past three years and alcohol no longer has any pull on me, as it used to. A lot of my recovery has to do with a desire for change and my spiritual needs to better my life.

I also may have subconsciously learned something from Sheree, my friend in New Jersey. Unfortunately, she, too, had a serious problem with alcohol. For many years, she was a victim of domestic abuse and turned to alcohol for relief. In 1999, I was shocked to receive a call from her mother, asking me to go to New Jersey.

Sheree's health had been declining since 1995 and in 1999, while drunk, she fell. Two days later, she had a seizure and went into a coma. The doctors declared her brain dead.

Because I was a funeral director/embalmer, Sheree's mother wanted me to help make the funeral arrangements and embalm Sheree's body. I took Matthew and Michael, who had grown up with Sheree and loved her like a second mom, and rushed to New Jersey, arriving only about eight hours after receiving Sheree's mom's call.

I met Sheree's family at the hospital, where my precious friend remained on life support. It was so very sad. Sheree was only forty-two years old and was the mother of seven children, ranging from five to seventeen years old. It was in the same month only three years earlier that Sheree had rushed to be by my side, as I struggled between life and death.

Unfortunately, Sheree's outcome wasn't to be as good as mine and so her doctors asked Sheree's mother and two oldest daughters if they would donate Sheree's organs. They asked for my thoughts and I told them that Sheree had been so loving in life, I was sure she would want to give of herself, to give the gift of life to others. They agreed.

I helped Sheree's family plan her funeral service and, after her body was released, I prepared it for burial. It was hard to handle a close friend's body, one I'd seen nurse so many babies and knew so well. It was also difficult because of the damage her head and face had suffered in her fall and as a result of the surgery to try to save her life. By the time I finished, Sheree looked pretty good, considering what she'd been through. But her lips were terribly swollen from the respirator and so, after saying their final, "goodbyes," her family decided on a closed casket for the public service.

Chapter 9

Of course, things weren't all bad in the years since John's attack on me. I had the joy of my new marriage to Richard even though we were unable to ever have a honeymoon or vacation due to the trials, surgeries and taking care of the boys. For the first few months when people asked me how I felt about the stab wounds, especially the one between my eyes, I would tell them that at least John didn't cut my eyes out and I can still see and watch as my boys grow into men. I also had the satisfaction of knowing I was helping other women. I was able to have the law changed so that all a woman had to do was request an order of protection if they felt threatened and they would be able to get one. Not like in my case where I had to have been physically hit first. Being told I would be killed did not count at that time in my county's handling of protective orders.

I was still plagued by the question of my purpose in life after losing what I felt God wanted me to do by losing my career so unfairly. I was still licensed but could not work in the city as it was too far away during the early years. I always felt I wasn't meant to exist, or so I thought since my adoption records were sealed and all I knew was I was a mistake and a "secret." Since I had survived many life-threatening events during my life, especially surviving the attempted murder, I just went back to wanting the stereotypical American life — married, two kids, white picket fence, etc.

It was on September 11, 2002, the one-year anniversary of the terrorist attack on the World Trade Center, that started the process of understanding my purpose in life. I was taking my youngest son, Michael, to a doctor's appointment in Richmond. On the way there, I was suddenly cut off by a car coming from the right-hand lane to make a left turn at the intersection. I was run out of my lane and into the left turn lane to avoid a collision with him. He stopped suddenly because the light was red and I skidded to a stop, just bumping his bumper. Three or four seconds later, the car behind us smashed into me because he was following too closely and going too fast.

Both of the other drivers received tickets, but I was the only one hurt in the accident. I was taken by ambulance to the hospital and checked out. They released me, but I suffered a herniated disc in my neck and one in my mid-back, between my shoulder blades.

The injury to the disc in my neck required having a bone plug put in between the two vertebrae, fusing them together, and a metal plate fixed in place to hold it all together. I then spent the time since in severe pain. I was awake sometimes at two in the morning and up for the day around four. I spent those hours looking back at my life and what I have been through. It was during the following year that I realized that God was telling me to use the life I lived and still have, to help others, which has always been what brought me the most joy.

I realized from my conception, God knew I would be one who would be attacked by the evil forces in the world. Good can come from bad things to bring glory to God for those who love the lord. God wants us to live a good life and live it more abundantly. John 10:10. I have learned that God has let me survive many horrible things. The latest physical damage done to my body happened on the date that it did as that date means to all of us the battle between "good and evil." I, an innocent victim hurt in the car accident, was like the people in the Twin Towers; the men who caused the accident were like the two airplanes. So the good that has come from another life-threatening event in my life is the fact that I have been blessed to understand my purpose and use it to bless others by writing this book.

I have learned through my life that it all starts with God. The purpose of your life is more important than just thinking about your own self-fulfillment, what you can own or buy, or what kind of great career you can have. If you want to know why you were born and have survived and why you have a kind of empty feeling inside that material things don't seem to fill, or drugs, sex, parties, etc., don't satisfy, then you need to look deeper.

The search for fulfillment has plagued mankind for thousands of years. If you only try to figure it out by looking at yourself and nothing else, you will fail. Philosophers have discussed and had heated debates about the meaning of life for many centuries, and to this day, none of them has come up with an answer. They only come up with guesses that come close to some into drugs, sex, and illegal activities. At one of the lowest points in his life, he was told about peoples' ideas of what it all might mean.

I met a nice gentleman a couple of years ago, who had tattoos all over his arms. He'd gotten into drugs, sex and all sorts of "bad" stuff. He ran into someone who told him about God and Jesus Christ and became interested in seeking more information about filling that void in his life that nothing else could fill. He told me the one thing that seems so simple that I must share it with you.

The simple meaning of what the letters that spell Bible stand for:

B   Basic
I   Instructions
B   Before
L   Leaving
E   Earth

I thought that was so amazing because in essence, it really is!

Your birth was not a mistake and your life is not a random happening. God made you for a reason. He planned when you would be born and decided how long you would live. You may think that you are in control of your life and that is partially true. You, by nature, have a mind that can make choices and everyone's life is driven by desire for something. Some people are driven only by material things while others are driven by guilt, anger or fear. You need to find out what it is that is driving your life and see what you are using to fill that void with.

Life is mostly about wanting to be loved and we all search for that. God wants us to value relationships and make every effort to maintain them, even when conflicts or problems arise. If you want peace and blessings in your life, you must first of all work to avoid conflicts.

To understand the whole picture, understand this. Everything comes from God. His goal is to show the universe his glory. The glory of God is to see who God is by seeing the essence of what he is. He is all-powerful. We see it everywhere, in the sky, in the clouds, in the ocean and the stars. Best of all, we see it when we realize that we can see it in ourselves! We are his best creation. We need to realize that our purpose in life is what God wants for us, not what we want for ourselves.

If you check your Bible, it plainly states, "And be not conformed to this world; but be ye transformed by the renewing of your mind, that ye may prove what is the good, and acceptable, and perfect, will of God." Romans 12:2

I have been in constant pain. In a way it has been a blessing. It has been the way that I have also been able to spend time looking and studying the condition of the nation, and the whole world situation.

We are fortunate to be living in the United States of America and most of us living here are citizens. Those who are not yet citizens are trying to achieve that goal and too many die in the attempt to get across the borders to gain entry into this country. This has been going on for centuries. The current uproar about the road to citizenship is a hurdle, that as a nation, we now have to tackle and one that needs to be done. But the history goes back to our country's start.

Most American settlers came here to escape religious persecution from European nations. Shortly after this, the basic American foundations were laid, based on Christian teachings. God was the basis for the Constitution and our freedoms. The common bond cemented the European Christians and also allowed other European religions the freedom to be practiced in this country without persecution. The Civil War and the issue of slavery split many denominations into different branches, but all are still united by the basic tenants of the Christian faith.

More Americans are church, synagogue, or mosque members, or affiliated with other religions, than ever before in our national history. The bewildering array of churches, sects, and cults should not mislead the student of the American religious scene. After all the denominations have been tallied, the fact remains that nine out of ten Americans belong to one of the six great denominational families: Baptist, Methodist, Lutheran, Episcopalian, Presbyterian (and Reformed), and the United Church of Christ.

Since its founding, the US has moved from a situation in which most of the states favored established Protestant churches to one of religious pluralism. At the time the Declaration of Independence was signed, Roman Catholics numbered only some 25,000 of the several million people in the new nation. Now Catholics constitute the largest single denomination in the US (about fifty-five million), and one out of every four Americans identifies himself as Catholic. The other religions have taken their place in a society once characterized as pan-Protestant: six million Jews, four million Eastern Orthodox, three million Latter-day Saints, and many others who identify themselves as secular humanists, Buddhists, Muslims, etc.

"To stay united, especially now, we must love one another, and to love one another we must know one another; to know one another, we must meet one another."

To meet those people whose beliefs and practices are different from your own, you must seriously study and sympathetically understand them if we, as a country, are going to move forward, without destroying what America originally stood for in the process.

We can hardly imagine what the world would be like if it had not been decisively influenced by descendants of a small Semitic tribe which took form more than three thousand years ago. From this group of people came the chief Western religions of Judaism, Christianity, and Islam.

Common sense would tell us that the Jews should have disappeared centuries ago. In the year AD 70, the Romans destroyed the Temple in Jerusalem and scattered the Jews throughout the world. Christians and Muslims tried to convert the Jews; many did accept the newer faiths, but millions kept their Jewish identity. Hitler murdered millions of Jews in what the Nazis called the "final solution" to the Jewish problem, but the Jews remain. In their darkest hours, the Jews looked for a Messiah who would usher in a new age for mankind.

About 2,029 years ago, a rabbi called himself that Messiah, gathered a band of followers, and was crucified. Most Jews rejected Jesus as the long-awaited Messiah, but his disciples established a sect within Judaism, what we now call Christianity. For a while, the Christians continued attending the synagogue, following the Jewish laws, and submitting to circumcision of infant baby boys. They finally broke away from Judaism and carried the Christian message to the Gentiles. They continue to use the Jewish scriptures, but added a New Testament.

Six centuries later, an Arabian teacher, Mohammed, also accepted the Old Testament and acknowledged the prophet-hood of Jesus. But they declared God, whom they call Allah, had a prophet and he was named Mohammed. He founded Islam, which has become another very large religion around the world and one that Americans have become very familiar with.

The Jihad, or Holy War, started in southern Arabia around the year AD 632. At that time, almost all Christian communities disappeared ahead of the Muslim advance. Islam means "to submit" to the will of God; Muslims object to being identified as Mohammedans, since they insist they follow God (Allah), rather than any man.

Muslims believe that God's final word to mankind is given in the Koran, which is very strict. A Muslim's religious life demands prayers five times a day. Muslims adore one God, living and enduring, merciful and all-powerful, very much as Christians do.

Our current world problems, and most of what is happening in American society, are all interrelated. Our morals and values have been declining for many years, since about the 1950s. But in the last thirty years, the decline has been more rapid. Satan, also called Lucifer, the fallen angel, has been determined to regain more control over God since the beginning of time.

God's plan is clearly stated in the Bible. "Thou was perfect in thy ways from the day that thou was created, till iniquity was found in thee. By the multitude of thy merchandise, they have filled the midst of thee with violence, and thou hast sinned; therefore, I will cast thee as profane out of the mountain of God; and I will destroy thee, O cowering cherub, from the midst of the stones of fire. Thou hast defiled thy sanctuaries by the multitude of thine iniquities, by the iniquity of thy traffic. Therefore will I bring forth a fire from the midst of thee, it shall devour thee, and I will bring thee to ashes upon the earth in the sight of all of them that behold thee. All they that know thee among the people shall be astonished at thee; thou shalt be a terror, and never shalt thou be any more." Ezekiel 28:15-19

Have you ever felt inadequate for the task to which God was calling you? Have you ever been confronted by a mountain of circumstances larger than any you have ever seen before? Have you ever stood alone in a situation where you felt outmatched, no matter which way you looked at it? Like there was no solution to your problem?

I think there have been times we have all felt like that and I know I have, many times. It is similar to what David in the Bible faced when he came up against Goliath. What God wants us to do as individuals is to put his purpose first in our lives and use his strength to achieve mastery over the giants in our lives.

God wants you not just to overcome one current problem, but to put your trust in him and praise him unashamedly, such that when you stand on top of your adversary, you will give God the glory for total victory. You can't be lukewarm about your religious convictions. You must feel strongly, one way or the other.

I think that we as a nation, in the past thirty years or so, have let our morals and values slide so far away from what is looked upon by God as being upright, that America is becoming a modern-day city of Sodom and Gomorrah. The Bible records that God destroyed these cities. If we as a nation, and each of us as individuals, do not do something to stop our downward slide, the evil in the world today, as evidenced by the terrorists attack on us on September 11, 2001, will continue and the end times are nearer than most people think. I will give you information to put a stop to this decline.

First, take a strong stand on your morals, values and religious convictions and speak about them to others. In Proverbs 18, there are many verses, some of which plainly spell it out: "Though a man desire having himself separated, but seeking wisdom, a fool hath no delight in understanding. The words of a man's mouth are as deep waters, and the wellspring of wisdom as a flowing brook. It is not good to accept the person of the wicked, to overthrow the righteous in judgment. A fool's mouth is his destruction, and his lips are the snare of his soul. The words of a talebearer are as wounds, and they go down into the innermost parts of the belly. Death and life are in the power of the tongue, and they that love it shall bear the fruit thereof."

Second, with the stand we take before we go out into our community, we must do our parts and affect our families and raise our children with correct morals and values. I think that's where this society in recent generations has gotten lazy. We must promote blessings to be carried down through the generations by starting with our children and ourselves. At home, follow these biblical teachings from Proverbs, chapters 12-17 and 24-26, as they are simple: "Apply thine heart unto instruction and thine ears to the words of knowledge. Withhold not correction from the child, for if thou beatest him with the rod, he shall not die. Thou shall use the rod, and shall deliver his soul from hell. For my son, if thine heart be wise, my heart shall rejoice, even mine. Yea, my reins shall rejoice, when the lips speak the right things. Father of the righteous shall greatly rejoice; and he that begetteth a wise child shall have joy of him. Thy father and thy mother shall be glad, and she that bare thee shall rejoice. My son, give me thine heart, and let thine eyes observe my ways." King James Version.

Raise up a child right, and he will have the right morals and values to affect this nation in the good and proper ways to shape the future. We need to be strong, as we are fighting against evil. Change starts with us, as it has since the founding of this country. Freedom does not come free and does not come without sacrifice. That means from you, too.

In the recent news, you can't have missed the fact that the battle is on for keeping the Ten Commandments and prayer in schools. Removing them further speeds our decline toward our nation's weakening. We must fight!

"Happy is the nation whose God is the Lord, the people He has chosen to be His own possession! The Lord looks down from heaven; He observes everyone. He gazes on all the inhabitants of the earth from His dwelling place. He alone crafts their hearts; He considers all their works. A king is not saved by a large army; a warrior will not be delivered by great strength. The horse is a false hope for safety; It provides no escape by its great power alone." Psalm 33:12-17

Also, take note of this — the battle is on both spiritually and literally for the land of Israel. It is the land that was promised by God to his people. It is getting very dangerous, not only for the region near Israel and the Middle East, but for us as Americans. We must protect Israel with all our heart and our government must stand by her. What is happening in Iran and Iraq with the proliferations of nuclear weapons is going to have a prophetic effect on the world. The condition of the nation and the whole world situation will have direct impacts on your life! I felt that I couldn't just sit by and do nothing, so I have researched and written this book because someone must take a stand.

Epilogue

My story continues, as does my healing. I have been blessed by God in that I've not lost my long-term memory, nor my artistic talents due to my severe head injury. When our garage was new the walls were bare and plain white. My husband Richard requested that I paint a mural in 1998 of the car he drove in his only Daytona 500 victory. The other things that Dale Earnhardt loved were fishing and hunting so I also painted a deer walking by a lake with a bass jumping out of the water. The garage got the title of the "official unofficial Dale Earnhardt museum" so in 2001 when Dale was killed in a crash at that very same track that he worked so hard to get his first win at, NBC and ABC news came out to videotape news stories about the garage/museum and the local newspaper came out and did a story about it also. I still have to paint Dale Jr's car on another wall and as I have stated earlier in my story when I set a goal I don't stop until that goal is accomplished. The "museum" is still a work in progress, as am I.

My mother moved from Virginia back to New Jersey, where she lives in a senior citizens development. She is surrounded by people her age and has access to senior services to help her with her needs, as I once had done for her. As a caregiver I was unable to keep up, considering my numerous surgeries during the period of time 1998 through 1999. Nowadays Jean, Richard's mother, who had lived alone next door, lives in the in-law apartment connected to our home. It is a very good situation for all of us. She is close, but still independent, and so are we.

As for the younger generation, Matthew is a trained professional chef, and Michael is out of school and trying to find a career. Richard's stepson, Tripp, from his second marriage, whom he raised since the age of four and who calls him "Dad" to this day, works at the family-owned business right down our road. My stepdaughter Caroline who has two daughters lives quite a few miles away but we get to see her every few months. I enjoy being a grandma and the girls are the daughters I never had.

Richard, Matt, Mike and I in 2001. God is our guide.

After searching for my birthparents for over twenty five years, I scraped together enough money from my disability income to do it, because I knew that life was too short to put it off any longer. Using the internet in 1998 I found my birthfather. Finding a male person is easier to do as their names do not change throughout life, and all I knew was my birthmother had named me at birth, and I guessed the last name she gave me had to be his. He was shocked, as he didn't even know I was born. He is a strict Catholic and he had trouble handling his feelings, such as that he had failed in his religious upbringing by not marrying my birthmother.

Nevertheless, we have developed a good relationship. A year after I contacted him, my birthfather and his wife came to visit my family and we had a nice time. My birthfather, with help from me, has come to look more deeply into the feelings he has about his faith, but still does not want to tell the rest of his family about me, other than his wife and sons as he feels that it is not necessary. My existence, however,

109

was a pleasant surprise for him, as I am his only daughter. He has three sons with his wife of over forty years.

I continued to search, used an investigator and got the supreme court of California to open the records for medical reasons. Right before Christmas 2005, I found my birthmother's family! It was a blessing, but also very sad. All my life, I was under the impression that I was a big secret and my birthmother had gone far away from where she was, all the way to California, to have me. Come to find out from her younger brother Alan, my uncle, that her family had known about my birth all along. They had planned my birthmother's long trip away to keep my birth a secret from her hometown so she wouldn't have a bad reputation there.

When Alan and I talked for the first time, he and his wife Martha were in tears. The family thought I had been lost to them forever. The sad part is that it was too late for me to ever meet my birthmother, as she died tragically in 1964, at the age of twenty-five. I just found out that my birthmother was the victim of a psychiatrist who was treating her for emotional reasons and took advantage of her emotional state by getting into a physical relationship with her. He broke the patient/doctor trust factor. Not only is that illegal but his emotional mistreatment of her as his patient came to a head when he not only dropped her suddenly as a "significant" other, where he had been telling her he was going to marry her, but also as a patient. All this was done to her by a letter!! This led her to commit suicide. I know how my birthmother felt as I went through the same thing with my boss. Someone who abuses their position of power to take advantage of someone's emotional weaknesses.

The different ways that each side of the family has dealt with and is feeling about me is so totally opposite, it is a confusing experience. However, it's also enriching, as I have longed for this knowledge my whole life. I did get to meet my whole maternal birth family in May 2006 when I went to Minnesota to meet them. It is like life has come full circle. My Uncle Alan, his wife Martha and all my cousins welcomed me with loving open arms. I have never felt so loved. God knows all and he has never failed me.

With all the events in my life up to this point, I have been blessed with the ability to now understand that each one of us is the most important person in our own world. Each one of us naturally feels that way, as it is human nature. In your own journey on the road of life that you will travel, I hope that after reading my story you will choose the right path. With the resources and information I provide along with the complete, up-to-date contact resources provided, you will have the confidence to put into action whatever it is that you need to do. Like me, you should now know that life is too short to waste time and put off things until tomorrow, because tomorrow is promised to no one. So use this guide right now. Don't suffer in silence because it will leave scars.

Information and Contact Guide

Controlling People

In my lifetime, I have encountered all types of controlling people, some worse than others. I dealt with John who, because of his low self-esteem issues, tried to control his surroundings. Our sons and I dealt with an emotional wall he had built to keep anyone from getting into his inner self and exposing what he felt were his shortcomings. He was very cold.

Domestic violence takes many forms. It can be emotional, verbal or physical. It can be against an adult or a child. However it is manifested, it all comes down to a desire for power and control.

My mother is a loving and very giving person, but having been ill with a lot of physical and emotional problems all of her life, she tries to control others by using guilt on them. That was extremely hard to live with in my case because, though my mother never said it directly, she would insinuate that I "owed" her more because I was adopted.

My mother-in-law, Jean, is a wonderful, kind person, but she grew up being responsible for her younger siblings and, thus, became independent and strong willed. Her own mother-in-law didn't like her for these qualities and in response, Jean became very assertive.

In our relationship, we have had a few times when I was at my weakest points, such as around the time of John's second criminal trial, when I begged for emotional help and abused alcohol to self medicate. Jean and I had some terrible encounters in which she yelled and tried to "shake some sense" into me, literally shaking me by the shoulders. I know she meant well, but sometimes she didn't understand how much I was suffering and that I really needed professional help, not criticism.

Richard is also a wonderful, kind and well-meaning person. His biggest problem in the control freak area is being what is called a Type A personality. He's a highly motivated and hard-working person and a perfectionist. He basically has a loud bark, but doesn't bite. My analogy is that he would be a perfect "junkyard dog" — scary to listen to, but has no teeth.

And like most people, I have run into the usual hot-tempered, "crazy" people who drive like they own the road. I just stay as far away as possible.

I am a very calm, non-confrontational type. If I have a problem and get angry, I bite my tongue and, like a duck, let it mostly slide off my back. If it's a real problem, I get my thoughts together and write them down, then send or give a letter to the person to get the issue out in the open, in hopes of resolving it.

The very act of someone trying to control you sends several negative messages: I don't trust you to do things right; I don't respect your judgment; I don't think you are competent; I don't value your insight (skill or experience). Have you found this to be true? You feel disrespected because the control freak seems to assume you know nothing. A control freak can rob you of your sense of confidence and self-control. Everything has to be just so. But why? Why can't he or she just live and let live?

Most controlling people are perfectionists and are obnoxious, tenacious, invasive, obsessive, critical, irritable, demanding, rigid, and close-minded. Noxious, in Latin, means hurtful. So it stands to reason that they injure almost every relationship they have because of their controlling and destructive ways. Stubborn is another way of describing them. They can be some of the most painfully critical people you will ever meet. They will judge others just as easily as a critic judges a movie. They somehow think that if they criticize others, it will make them better or a situation improve. A control freaks is a faultfinder who has one sharp eye for faults and one blind eye for virtues.

Control freaks are known to be what is called a Type A personality. Their notorious need for control correlates with a high risk for developing heart disease. Richard has already had three heart attacks and borders on possible bypass surgery.

The driving force behind a control freak is rooted in low self-esteem and/or anxiety. Anxiety isn't all bad. Without it, there would be no growth or progress in all of us. Right after birth, anxiety provides us with the motivation to act to get what we want. But it is when the level of anxiety is out of proportion to the situation that trouble begins. Control freaks don't know when and where to stop.

You will have control freaks all around you in life, whether as co-workers, bosses, family members or acquaintances. If you are married to one, that can become a very serious issue. Unfortunately, home is where spouses feel they can get away with having total control, so they feel secure doing it.

The first thing you must do if you are dealing with a controlling spouse is confront the issue and put the problem on the table. It may seem obvious to some, but it isn't always to others. Besides, it's easier to avoid conflict. I suggest the following: Don't try to "one up" your spouse by keeping score; Compromise and negotiate a solution; Don't point fingers at each other; Pinpoint what is most important and try to resolve it; Most of all, "fight fair." This means don't belittle the other person or his or her opinion; don't become a "victim" or play the blame game.

But what if you're the controlling person? Life today means we are time-starved. We race into the day and try to do more than we have hours in the day. We plan for what we want to do in the future and try to control what has not even happened, not just tomorrow, but up to next month or next year. We can easily lose our perspective. We then blame ourselves for what doesn't get accomplished or isn't done right. Negative self-talk is common. Some safeguards to help you keep from spinning out of control or to get you back from the abyss if you are there are these: Lower your anxiety level; Unwind and slow down; Give others tasks to do; Don't get trapped in the "what if" mind game.

Additionally, you must work on repairing, if possible, the damage you have done to yourself and those around you. Admit you were wrong and ask for forgiveness from those you have hurt.

Grace is a gift from God that enables us to sooth our hurting souls. Realize that you do not have power to control the future. Trust God to control it for you and the anxiety level inside you will greatly diminish.

How to Not be Stressed Out, Anxious and Fearful

We all struggle with the demands of daily life, which is hectic and can be confusing, considering all the difficult decisions we have to make. When we make bad choices, we sometimes blame the devil and say, "the devil made me do it." Well, think about that. Satan's job is to destroy. He does that by giving you wrong thoughts.

These thoughts, whether about your job, family or friends, can lead you into thinking things that might happen, but have not yet happened, which is called imagination. When you start to imagine the "what ifs," you will

115

start to get stressed because you think the worst and get fearful. Anxiety is a bewildering and sometimes terrifying feeling of being out of control. You must believe and trust that God is in control, or you will let yourself spin wildly out to who knows where and that can be disastrous.

You must not let circumstances shake your direction or your choices when you are under stress. I know it greatly affected me when I was being tossed between my emotionally abusive husband at home and sexual misconduct at work.

Please try to use these verses from the best guide for life there is, the Bible. "Let not your heart be troubled; ye believe also in me." John 14:1 "Peace I leave with you, my peace I give unto you; not as the world giveth, give I unto you. Let not your heart be troubled, neither let it be afraid." John 14:27 "Finally, my brethren, be strong in the Lord, and in the power of his might." Ephesians 6:10 "Put on the whole armour of God, that ye may be able to stand against the wile of the devil." Ephesians 6:11 "Above all, taking the shield of faith, wherewith ye shall be able to quench all the fiery darts of the wicked." Ephesians 6:16

See the Resource Guide and Information for resources to help you make good choices and not succumb to stress.

How to Have Faith and Hope and Battle Depression

No one ever promised that life would be a rose garden. Sometimes we have all heard that "life is like a bowl of cherries and all I get are the pits." I have personally had many, many times in my life when things went terribly wrong and out of my control. I used to say, "Wasn't God supposed to not overload your boat and cause it to sink, 'cause I really feel like mine is going to?" Well, that was well before some of the major traumas and crises happened in my life.

For most of us, we need to have faith in God. Faith in

God comes by hearing his word. All of us are spiritual beings. To be spiritual beings implies belief in a power greater than ourselves. It means that life is sacred and has been given to us as a gift. It is easy to lose sight of the spiritual dimension of life. We struggle with jobs that burn us out, forgetting that work, envisioned by the sixteenth-century theologian John Calvin, is innately good, even holy. We build plans for our future, but forget that, ultimately, the only security that any of us has rests deep within the quietness of our beings.

Fortunately, there is a growing desire to better understand the spiritual dimension of life. New studies aptly demonstrate that the religious pulse of the American people is quickening. A *US News and World Report* survey discovered that Americans are becoming more aggressive in proclaiming that spirituality "is the root of their very existence." Regardless of the religious orientation, it has been discovered there is one important fact — faith has a powerful effect in helping people recover a sense of balance, tranquility, and hope.

The first thing you must do is, count your blessings. Even when things may be going horribly wrong, you should not let a day go by without taking time to appreciate God's gifts. You can stop Satan in his tracks and from wreaking havoc in your life and making a bad situation worse by looking in the Bible. "Out of the mouth of babes and sucklings hast thou ordained strength because of thine enemies, that thou mightest still the enemy and the avenger." Psalm 8:2 That makes Satan be just like a fish out of water.

I found this to be so true right after I was almost murdered and lost my home and my job, all in the space of less than a month. I had every reason to lose hope and faith and get depressed, and for about two days I was so terribly lost.

But it seemed that God stepped in. Jean cared for me after I came out of the hospital so that my boys, disabled mother, and I had shelter over our heads and food to sustain us. The Bible says, "Be careful of nothing; but in everything by prayer and supplication with thanksgiving let you requests be made known unto God." Philippians 4:6

Then Richard gave us his home to move into and he lived with his mother until we got married five months later. We got married sort of in secret, since John was still walking free and we all lived in fear of him, but I felt that God had even chosen our wedding date. We snuck it in on February 1, 1997. The month and day numbers are two and one, which come from Genesis 2:24. God describes marriage as a union in which two become one.

We must have faith, and who better to have faith in than God, the one who made us? Faith means trust. I had spent twenty years searching for my birthfather. I found him after my attack by using the Internet, which has been a wonderful experience. But I realized that, after everything I have been through, by my faith and putting my trust in God, my father God has always been with me.

We hope for good things to happen to us, as I did even in the midst of terrible circumstances. I had to trust that God knew what was going to happen, but at times it wasn't easy.

Here is a way for you to grasp what faith and hope are based on:

T   Take time to pray.
R   Rest in his peace.
U   Understand his teaching.
S   Stand firm in his word.
T   Tell others

I know all too well that many of you are dealing with depression. I, too, have gone through periods of it and it's not anywhere you want to be. I was very depressed at the loss of my career because it was what I felt God had meant for me to do with my life and I had worked so hard to earn my license. At the same time, I was dealing with the real issue of a severe brain injury, which affects the brain chemistry and how it alters your moods.

I had to keep telling myself that I was thankful for surviving the attack, thankful that I was not a vegetable, as the doctors said I might be, or didn't have difficulty walking. People would tell me in kindness that God closes one door, but opens a window. That's true, but to get to the window, you have to travel down a long hallway and that hallway is called depression and it is dark and lonely.

I did find that my sense of humor was still intact. When people would ask me how things were for me, and given that I had just become a licensed funeral director, I would reply, "Everything is looking up and at least it's not from six feet under!" Or, after I had one of the reconstructive surgeries that left two screws about a quarter-inch long sticking out of my head for three weeks, I would show them to people and joke, "Don't you ever let anyone tell you that I have a screw loose. Mine are tight!" They would just laugh so much that it kept me feeling quite upbeat, also.

As soon as I felt a bit better, about six months after I got out of the hospital, I turned my thoughts to some way that I could still help others. If I couldn't work as a funeral director, helping people in that type of crisis situation, it occurred to me that my own crisis of domestic violence would be an area in which I could help others. So I focused on what programs there were in my local area and, to my amazement, found there were none.

I put my mind to work and God stepped in again. I happened to see *People* magazine in the grocery store that week and on the cover, a headline caught my eye. It said, "The Victim's Voice." I bought the magazine, and to my complete surprise, it was a story about a woman who, like me, had almost been killed by her ex-boyfriend. She had been shot in the back and is permanently paralyzed, but she turned her life into a quest to help others like her. I was determined to do the same and since we had no help for

ᵗʰᵉNews Journal

October 14 - 20, 1997

SURVIVORS. Domestic violence can inflict lifelong scars on its victims and their children. Diane Arias, Mary Ann Worsham and Leonora Peabody have formed a Powhatan support group called Citizens Against Domestic Violence.

Domestic violence:surviving the system

Editor's note: In a three-part series, The News Journal explores the faces of domestic violence in rural counties—from women who have survived it and who are determined to make the road to recovery easier for others.

By Nancy Crowder Chaplin
"The system does not work." The statement is made with slow and deliberate emphasis by Diane Arias.

Arias works for the Powhatan Social Services Department as a section 8 housing coordinator. She is also on the task force of the Powhatan/Goochland Citizens Against Domestic Violence, which her agency is supporting as a part of their general social services mission.

"The system" which Arias speaks of encompasses the range of response or lack of response to domestic violence victims— from law

Series

enforcement officers, to judicial intervention officials— and the attendant bureaucratic obstacle course to ultimate protective orders and safety— to the lack of support services in the counties. Arias is a victim and survivor of domestic violence.

Arias comes to the interview with a co-worker and friend, Leonora Peabody. She also works

"It was my Vietnam conflict."
-Leonora Peabody about her abuse.

for the department as a welfare/workfare view coordinator. Peabody is also on the task force of the Citizens Against Domestic Violence. She is a survivor of 17 years of domestic abuse. "It was my Vietnam conflict," she says in a measured and precise voice.

Nancy Crowder Chaplin, "Domestic Violence: Surviving the System,"
Amelia News Journal, October 14, 1997.

Violence

Continued from page 1

Arias and Peabody meet Mary Ann Worsham for the first time, although they know who she is. As victims of domestic violence they have closely followed the story of Worsham, whose ex-husband was convicted in July for an assault so vicious it left Worsham unconscious in a blood-soaked bed until she was discovered by her children hours after the attack. It also left her with permanent partial paralysis and in need of continuing reconstructive surgery. Now remarried, she has recently started a small business designing and selling memorial stones.

Worsham admits the violence she suffered did not follow the typical progressive pattern of abuse. In fact, her assault was the first instance of physical abuse— although there was psychological abuse including threats and verbal harassment.

Worsham brought a scrapbook she made which contained newspaper articles, crime scene photographs, and medical records, including a brain scan that revealed fissures in her skull.

"It was therapeutic for me to do this," she says of the book. "Putting all this in a book is a way of saying, 'I can close this book.'" Worsham finds meaning in the name the Citizens Against Domestic Violence has decided to give their initial efforts— "Project Horizon."

"That's important," Worsham says. "You have to encourage victims to look beyond."

Worsham's eagerness to become involved with helping domestic violence victims lead to gentle, but articulately stated words of caution from Peabody to "make sure you're ready."

There is instant rapport between the women— an empathetic flow that needs no prodding from the interviewer for facts and feelings to spill forth.

Are tales of domestic abuse the female equivalent to more typically masculine "war stories?" It's a chilling thought. Some parallels can be drawn.

There is pride in survival— even triumph. "I'm here. I'm whole. I made it." There is keen awareness that others, like Nicole Simpson, didn't survive. "There but for the grace of God..." say some victims.

There is guilt, pain, and regret for the most innocent victims— the children— of each woman's domestic battlefield. Their children's psychological scars are each woman's ongoing reminder of past episodes that can never entirely be forgotten.

There is a missing element to the "war story" analogy, however. There is no bravado. Pride, yes. Bravado, no. Bravado is an aggressive trait and the word that surfaces again and again in the free-flowing conversation of these women is bravado's antonym— *"passive."*

"I grew up in a big rural, fighting family," said Peabody. "Everybody fought, including the women. The women in my family fought back— they gave as good as they got. But, for some reason, I was different. I just never wanted to hurt anybody. I was passive."

Peabody says she accepted violence as normal. She admitted she "picked" violent men. She is happily married now, although she admits certain vulnerabilities— like hostility— that surfaced with therapy. "I'm a very hostile person," she says. "I work on that."

Peabody tells a brief story of a point in her recovery where she thought she was ready to take on the responsibility of leadership in the cause of helping domestic violence survivors, but then realized she was still too tender and reactive. Of the three women she has had the most time to heal. Worsham's ordeal is more recent, but the trial and conviction of John Warmoth has provided closure and safety.

Aria's encounter with domestic violence is the most recent. It is a violence less severe in terms of actual physical trauma, but perhaps more typical of domestic violence situations in general. It is a case where a woman has no battle wounds to reveal— no blood, stab wounds, broken bones, or burns— but the fear and terror a mentally unstable partner can inflict falls in the spectrum of domestic violence.

Even with physical evidence of flesh wounds, the wheels of justice grind slow. "Criminal justice system means justice for criminals," Worsham mutters in a cynical outburst.

Without flesh wounds, seeking protection from a harassing and abusive spouse is more difficult— difficult to the point of being abuse in itself, as Arias has found.

A support group for victims of domestic violence has started. One ultimate dream the group has is a shelter for battered spouses.

domestic violence victims in my area, I had to do something about it.

Then, to my surprise again, the woman featured in the magazine was coming to Virginia Beach to speak the following week! I needed to meet her and learn whatever I could, so I would be able to start a taskforce and support group. I wanted to change the laws about restraining orders, especially because I was unable to get one when I requested it. I also wanted to get whatever strength from her I could, so I would be able to make it through the upcoming criminal trial, which was only weeks away.

I found that if you focus on the positive things in your life, it helps you take your mind off the negative. It enables you to move past the darkness in the hallway called depression. Helping others doesn't have to be anything big. It can be a card, a telephone call, or an e-mail.

The Bible again says about depression, "A merry heart doeth good like medicine; but a broken spirit drieth the bones." Proverbs17:22 and, "Then he said unto them, 'Go your way, eat the fat, and drink the sweet, and send portions unto them for whom nothing is prepared; for this day is holy unto our Lord; neither be ye sorry; for the joy of the Lord is your strength.'" Nehemiah 8:10

You see that, as the guide of your life, the Bible teaches that we need to focus not on ourselves, but outside of ourselves, and we will be fulfilled. I have found this to be the biggest truth in my life.

Don't misunderstand me. I do understand firsthand that depression is a medical condition that, if left untreated, can be deadly. You and your loved ones must treat it as such and seek help for it. I just feel that mind over matter is sometimes stronger than medicine and has been in my case.

Over the years, I have also found comfort in music. Here is a list of songs and the artists who perform them that I think apply to the subjects we've been discussing: *God's Unanswered Prayers*, Garth Brooks; *I Hope You Dance*,

Leanne Womack; *Three Wooden Crosses*, Randy Travis; *Live Like You Were Dying*, Tim McGraw; *If Nobody Believed in You*, Joe Nichols; *Long Black Train*, Josh Turner; *Paper Angels*, Jimmy Wayne.

There are also numerous resources for dealing with depression and many of them are listed in the Resource Guide and Information.

How to Forgive Others

I'm sure you have heard the saying "forgive and forget," right? I know I have.

All through our lives, as we grow up, other people hurt our feelings or do bad things to us. We get mad, yell at them or cry, etc. As we age, we try to get control of our emotions and mature. Part of that maturity is learning about not "sweating the small stuff." Yes, sometimes people do things to us that are truly awful and we don't know if we can ever rid ourselves of the pain or anger that the event has inflicted on us.

At times we live in the past, never getting over the anger or pain. We desire to rewrite our personal histories; that is so powerful because we become overwhelmed by the fact that it can't be done. How do you let go? Bitterness is a normal feeling to have, but you should go through it, not live in it. The burden of it will eat you alive, as I learned.

From 1999 through 2000, I couldn't get the memories and the emotions that went along with what I had been through to stop replaying in my mind. Having to go through a second criminal trial contributed to this situation by forcing me to relive all the memories. With post-traumatic stress disorder, I was under so much pressure at that time that I turned to alcohol to dull my everyday stress. That was not a good choice at all, but it was the only thing that totally eliminated the horrific things I was being put through.

The law was forcing me to relive everything and if I refused, I would be breaking the law. So each day and night, the attack and all the emotions were there and being drunk made it bearable. Being a drunk, though, is the worst thing anyone can do to herself and her marriage and children. I was on the verge of suicide and my family couldn't understand why. They just said, "be strong," and thought that was enough.

The hardest things for me to forgive were first, that my boss had used religion as one of the tools to put pressure on me to be physical with him. My spiritual relationship with God and Jesus was so strong and my morals were such that using religion was the lowest thing any human being could have done to me. Second, the use of his position while I was doing my internship (which was required by law) was another tool he used. Then, I was so hurt by how my boss "kicked me while I was down" when he fired me. That was the hardest thing for me. He had unfairly taken away the career I had worked so hard for and felt that God had wanted for me. So trying to forgive him took me the longest.

Third, in the small county where I live, the trials were front-page news, as they were in area counties and the big city, also. But I encountered what is called "media bias." The county newspaper covered the trials well, but left out one important piece of information that was one-sided and was hurtful to me. The details of both trials were reported somewhat accurately, except that they stated that I had no memory of the attack which I did and the name of the person whom I had been physical with was not printed. All the other papers did print Matt's name, except the paper for the county where I worked and lived. The reason was that David, the publisher, was Matt's best friend and he didn't want Matt's name mentioned to protect his reputation. Well, what about mine?

There were many more terrible things that were said and done to me during the time from 1995 through 2000, when I really began the forgiveness process. I thought that to forgive someone, I would get a "feeling," like I would somehow feel an emotion of forgiveness and it would just happen. Well, I was wrong. You see, forgiveness is a choice.

Forgiveness means facing a wrongdoing, experiencing the feelings connected with being wronged and, after a period of time that only you can determine, letting go of actively holding the wrongdoing against the person or persons. The result is a restoration of your general sense of trust and love and a feeling of peacefulness. In the Bible, many verses are connected to forgiveness. "Not rendering evil for evil, or railing for railing; but contrariwise blessing; knowing that ye are thereunto called, that ye should inherit a blessing." 1 Peter: 3-9

Also we are told to "turn the other cheek." As hard as it is to believe, forgiving and praising God when times are tough really do make your life better. Consider the example of Jesus's disciples, Paul and Silas, who during their imprisonment and beatings were thankful and praising God. "And at midnight Paul and Silas prayed, and sang praises unto God; and the foundations of the prison were shaken; and immediately all the doors were opened, and everyone's bands were loosed." Acts 16:20-25 Forgiveness gives freedom.

As I learned, it is essential to recognize that forgiveness has its own timetable. It cannot be pushed. Premature forgiveness can backfire and not work and will leave you frustrated. Well-intentioned friends may urge you to "let bygones be bygones," but their comments often reflect their feelings, rather than your needs. You were pressured enough growing up, so don't pressure yourself into forgiving before you are ready.

I have gotten to a place where I am so at peace that my family and friends are still in awe and some are upset at me because I have forgiven John for trying to murder me;

I was able to do that back in 2000. I felt that he had taken enough of my life by permanently disabling me and I suffer every day, so why should I give him any more of me by letting my emotions suffer also?

My ex-in-laws, my son's grandparents, still don't believe that their son committed the crime, but my ex-father-in-law and I have a nice, civil relationship. We can talk about whatever needs to be said and we share a common love, for the boys. I send over tomatoes and squash from my garden to them because I like to share and I will always care about what we shared in the past, even though they hid and hold the money that John owes me for child support and from the civil trial. I forgave them as well.

Since day one of being attacked, my main concern was the mental and physical health of my sons. I have not once badmouthed John (Daddy) to them, because that would hurt them. It was very hard, especially since I heard through the boys every time they were with their father the lies, badmouthing, and horrible things that he was saying and doing to them. I knew that, sometime in the future, it would matter what I said and did and I was not the kind of person to lower myself to his level.

As far as my ex-mother-in-law goes, I believe that all things work for the greater good for those who love the Lord. For many years, my mother-in-law wouldn't talk to me. Unlike her husband, she couldn't have a civil relationship with me. But God does change hearts.

In March 2006, Richard had to have another stent put in his heart. It makes his fourth. I had heard from my boys that my ex-father-in-law had chest pains the day before and I was worried about him. While at the hospital with Richard, my older son, Matthew, and I went upstairs for a little while and visited my ex-father-in-law. When coming out of the unit, we came face-to-face with my ex-mother-in-law. She and I smiled at each other and talked for a couple of minutes.

About three days later, I called her on the phone and asked how her husband was. She and I talked for about fifteen minutes. It seems that, even though she doesn't know the truth about what her son did, she knows that I have not turned the boys against her and her husband because they love them and are helping her, now that she needs them to drive her to the hospital, etc. She and I can now somewhat return to a relationship of common connection, due to the love of the boys and the fact that I have never poisoned their feelings for their father or their grandparents.

Check the Resource Guide and Information for web sites and phone numbers of organizations that can help you learn to forgive and let go of your anger and pain.

Celebrate The Road to Recovery
Eight Principles Based on the Beatitudes

Realize I'm not God. I admit that I am powerless to control my tendency to do the wrong thing and that my life is unmanageable.

Happy are those who know they are spiritually poor.

Earnestly believe that God exists, that I matter to Him, and that he has the power to help me recover.

Happy are those who mourn, for they shall be comforted.

Consciously choose to commit all my life and will to Christ's care and control.

Happy are the meek.

Openly examine and confess my faults to myself, to God, and to someone I trust.

Happy are the pure in heart.

Voluntarily submit to every change God wants to make in my life and humbly ask Him to remove my character defects.

Happy are those whose greatest desire is to do what God requires.

Evaluate all my relationships. Offer forgiveness to those who have hurt me and make amends for harm I've done to others, except when to do so would harm them or others.

Happy are the merciful. Happy are the peacemakers.

Reserve a daily time with God for self-examination, Bible reading, and prayer in order to know God and His will for my life and to gain the power to follow His will.

Yield myself to God to be used to bring this Good News to others, both by my example and by my words.

Happy are those who are persecuted because they do what God requires.

"Celebrate the Road to Recovery," handout from the Red Lane Baptist Church. Printed with permission.

129

Mary Ann Worsham

Abortion / Adoption

Living through the loss of a baby I would never hold in my arms raised some issues for me, some that I had pushed to the back of my mind and some that I hadn't fully considered before. The 1973 Roe vs. Wade decision to legalize abortion changed the options pregnant women had. I was thirteen when the ruling was made and, like most teens, didn't give it much thought. Now I wondered, if abortion had been legal fifteen years earlier, what decision would my birthmother have made?

From my own miscarriage at thirteen weeks, I learned that a human being has everything needed for life, such as arms, legs, brain and a heart, by ten weeks gestation. With my new understanding of the whole situation, I, as do many other people, believe life begins at conception, though that statement has been the basis for heated debate for decades. I feel that abortion is plain and simply the murder of an innocent life. With today's technology, a fetus can survive if born prematurely, when just decades ago it could not. Furthermore, the extremely inhumane type of abortion called "partial birth abortion" is simply murder of a fully capable infant who can survive outside the womb, but has its brain sucked out before the head is delivered!

You would not be reading this if I had been aborted. Every decision we make as human beings has consequences. To abort a child has a ripple effect, like throwing a rock into a pond. It hits in one place, but its effects spread out in rings, wider and wider as they go. That's how life is and whatever we do, we affect our surroundings.

I encourage all women to think about what they do and give the gift of life if they find themselves in the position of an unexpected pregnancy. If a pregnancy is the result of incest or rape, there are groups that can help women deal with that without an abortion, but each case is very difficult, to say the least.

If the situation is one where the mother's life is in danger, it may come to the point where it is necessary to end the pregnancy. In that case, I feel the mother's life comes first, but all efforts should be made to save both. If you do not want the child, give it away and don't burden yourself. Look at it as a gift to someone else. It truly is, because there are so many people who want and can't have children of their own. Call your local adoption agency or look in the newspaper; there are ads placed by people looking for infants all the time. You may also consider the resources contained here.

Pregnant and scared? Considering getting an abortion? Go to www.thinkaboutitonline.com. Had an abortion and need help? Go to www.operationoutcry.org.

Considering adoption? Start with www.adoption.com. Place here the list of additional web sites that are on the disc.

You can also write to:
Committee for Persons Wishing To Adopt
P.O. Box 4074
Chevy Chase, MD 20815.

Remember that you may be surprised by what will happen in the future if you give what is growing inside of you a chance. He or she has a future too. God bless you and your decision. American Adoptions

Find the answers to all your **adoption** questions. Sponsored by: http://www.americanadoptions.com/ [Found on Web Search Picks]

International Adoption – Christian Agency

131

America World Adoption Association is a licensed Christian agency dedicated to helping families adopt internationally. Dependable, personal service. We have placed over 1000 children.
Sponsored by: http://awaa.org [Found on Overture]

Adoption
Courageous Women Choose **Adoption**. Call Toll Free 24 Hours a Day.
Sponsored by: http://www.AdoptionsaChoice.com// [Found on Web Search Picks]

National **Adoptions** Center – **Adoption** Information and **Adoption**...
The National **Adoption** Center brings children on-line through photographs and descriptions and offers a wealth of information that will help you learn more about...
http://www.adopt.org/ [Found on Google, Ask Jeeves, Yahoo!]

Adopting.com – Internet **Adoption** Resources
Help for adoptive parents and birth parents in the processes of adopting a child is in the comprehensive listing of **adoption** resources on the...
http://www.adopting.com/ [Found on Ask Jeeves, Yahoo!, LookSmart]
Independent **Adoption** Center
Free to birthmothers. Affordable open **adoption** and home study services. Licensed agency.
Sponsored by: http://www.adoptionhelp.org [Found on Overture, Ask Jeeves, Yahoo!]

Adopting.org: Adopt a Baby, Child, Infants, Kids, Older, Services...
Adopting.org is your destination for everything **adoption**. Find waiting children or an **adoption** agency. ...

Baby names. **Adoption** laws. Featured **Adoption** Products...
http://www.adopting.org/ [Found on Google, Ask Jeeves, Yahoo!]

Center for Family Building
If you are pregnant and considering **adoption**, find adoptive parents here. Quality resources for birthparents.
Sponsored by: http://www.centerforfamily.com [Found on Overture]

Pregnant? Consider **Adoption**
American Adoptions provides a full range of services to adoptive families and birth parents across the country, including Augusta. Over 300 adoptions annually, 24-hour toll-free help line.
Sponsored by: http://www.americanadoptions.com [Found on Overture, FindWhat, Enhance Interactive, Ask Jeeves]

Considering **Adoption?**
Unplanned pregnancy? There is help. Scared? Alone? Courageous Choice will guide you through **adoption** with complete support. You are not alone. Call and speak to a counselor today.
Sponsored by: http://courageouschoice.com [Found on Overture]
BirthMothersOptions.com – Great Resource
A helpful support site for birth mothers considering **adoption**. Find valuable information about your options, rights and more to make a sound decision about your baby's future.
Sponsored by: http://www.birthmothersoptions.com [Found on Overture]

Children's Hope International **Adoption**
Respected, licensed and accredited, CHI places about

800 children in all states from China, Russia, Kazakh-
stan, Colombia, Guatemala, India, Nepal and Vietnam.
Free **adoption** guide online.
Sponsored by: http://childrenshopeint.org [Found on
Overture]

International **Adoption** by Shepherd Care
A Christian **adoption** agency in Florida, **Adoption** by
Shepherd Care provides **adoption** placement services
for children from foreign countries such as Russian,
Romania, Poland, Guatemala and China.
Sponsored by: www.adoptionshepherdcare.com [Found
on WebCatalog]

Miscarriage / Loss of a Child

When I worked at a funeral home, I was able to draw
on my miscarriage experience to guide me when I helped
people who lost their children. One couple lost a child at
seven months gestation, two months before it was to be
born. They wanted the baby to be embalmed and put into
a small child's casket. A few couples lost infants at birth
or under the age of one year old. These were especially
hard funerals because it goes against the "natural order"
of things for a parent to lose a child. I also helped families
who lost teenagers. One was a car accident, one a suicide,
one was hit by a car while riding an off-road vehicle, and
the other was a murder.

For the families of these children, especially the parents,
they were in the first stage of the grief process when I dealt
with them. This was shock, unbearable sadness, anger, and
a feeling of hopelessness. I tried to comfort them the best
way I could, which was what they needed at that time.

I think the most important thing to remember is to treat

134

people the same way I would want to be treated. I found that if I saw them later, it meant a lot to them for me to mention in conversation the child they'd lost. They knew the child was not completely gone or forgotten.

Each couple is different and I took that into consideration of course, but to pretend that the loss never happened is to deny the people involved the ability to go through the grieving process with the support they need from others.

Compassionate Friends
Online at www.CompassionateFriends.org

Or write for information at
Compassionate Friends
P.O. Box 3696
Oak Brook, IL 60522-3696

Or call them toll free at 1-877-969-0010

From notes taken by Mary Ann Worsham during a class on death, dying, and the grieving process at John Tyler Community College:

The Truth Is...

The truth ISN'T that you will fell "all better" in a couple of days, or weeks, or even months.

The truth IS that the days will be filled with an unending ache and the nights will feel one million sad years long for a while. Healing is attained only after the slow necessary progression through the stages of grief and mourning.

The truth isn't that a new pregnancy will help you forget.

The truth is that, while thoughts of a new pregnancy soon may provide hope, a lost infant deserves to be mourned just as you would have with anyone you loved. Grieving takes a lot of energy and can be both emotionally and physically draining. This could have an impact upon your health during another pregnancy. While the decision to try again is a very individualized one, being pregnant while still actively grieving is very difficult.

The truth isn't that grieving is morbid, or a sign of weakness or mental instability.

The truth is that grieving is work that must be done. Now is the appropriate time. Allow yourself the time. Feel it, flow with it. Try not to fight it too often. It will get easier if you expect that it is variable, that some days are better than others. Be patient with yourself. There are no short cuts to healing. The active grieving will be over when all the work is done.

Characteristics of a Crisis

There are six characteristics of a crisis.

FIRST: A crisis hits suddenly, without warning. It often strikes at a point in life in which everything is going well. In the moments after it strikes, we are stunned as we seek to comprehend what has happened. The very first words spoken are usually, "I can't believe it." When it happens, we don't usually have the luxury of sitting back in a detached manner to analyze our options. Our whole beings become absorbed in the event.

SECOND: It threatens our security. Crisis situations cause us to panic because we might lose something very precious, something that has given structure, meaning and purpose to our lives.

THIRD: Its resolution is unpredictable. There's an element of uncertainty in all situations. We simply do not know how things are going to work out. We like to believe that we can weather the storm, but in our quiet moments, we wonder if we can. This element of unpredictability is the most unsettling part.

FOURTH: It presents dilemmas. Dilemmas arise because there are no clear-cut solutions to difficult problems. A decision that you think will help the problem is not always successful. Sometimes we are forced to make decisions on issues about which we have little or no knowledge and in which we have little experience.

FIFTH: It erodes self-confidence. Why do we feel less confident? Because everything I have just listed takes a cumulative toll on a person's outlook. The sudden impact of a negative event reminds us that life is fragile. The unpredictability of the outcome leaves us unsettled. This causes anxiety. The result is that there may be an apprehension about life that was not there before the event or events. Does that old self-confidence ever return? This brings us to the next characteristic of a crisis.

SIXTH: A crisis also leaves a hopeful legacy. This is where survivors of a traumatic event step forward. It is not a short process, but looking forward to a better future is the first step of coping and healing.

Some web sites you may find helpful include: www. crisishelp.org, www.crisishelp.com, www.crsishelp.us/site/ uscc, and www.sickchicks.homestead.com/crisishelp.html (for women with disabilities who are experiencing a crisis and may be severely isolated).

Natural Disasters

If and when the time comes that you are faced with any sort of natural disaster, the first thing to remember is to remain calm. Panic is the worst thing that can happen, as you will not be able to think in a practical way to get out of harm's way and get help if needed.

You also need to be prepared before an event occurs, rather than waiting until it has arrived to figure out what you will do. To begin with, make sure you are properly insured. You should also know the characteristics of the environment where you live, such as the area's terrain, including hills, cliffs, rivers, drainage, etc. And know what weather occurrences are typical for your area. Tornadoes? Hurricanes? Severe thunderstorms?

Next, every home should have a first aid kit. Fire extinguishers are also a must and you should have a few gallons of fresh drinking water on hand.

Once the weather has become threatening, as long as you have electricity and it's safe to use it, keep track of what's going on weather-wise by listening to television and radio. Also, you can get a lot of detailed information on the Internet by going to www.nws.noaa.gov-national.

Post emergency numbers near all phones in your house. Also post numbers of friends and family members. Have a plan for the family in case of needing a quick escape.

For immediate help when a disaster has struck, call the American Red Cross at 1-202-303-4498.

Helpful toll-free numbers include: General Government Information, 1-800-688-9889 and Environmental Protection Agency, 1-800-438-2474.

Great web sites for information include WWW.READY. GOV and WWW.FIRSTGOV.GOV.

To make sure your pet is protected, go to www.hsus.org for Pet Disaster Preparedness.

Eating Disorders

Bulimia and anorexia are known as eating disorders and, unfortunately, are not uncommon. They are especially prevalent in adolescent girls and women. I know that sometimes we want to control things, especially as teens, when so much seems beyond our control. Our eating habits are an easy area where we can exert control, but taking it too far can be dangerous. You can encounter severe problems, such as the enamel on your teeth being eaten away by stomach acid when you vomit and ulcers in you throat and mouth. Also, you lose nutrients when you don't ingest the proper amounts of food and this can kill you!

If you do what I did, it is something you can control. Don't let it control you. At the same time, it's not unusual to need help and you shouldn't feel bad if you do. I encourage you to talk to your friends, school counselors or teachers. You can also look in your local phone book for doctors or others who can help you, or consult the information below. Knowledge of both conditions is widespread and help is available, but you need to get it before it's too late.

As a parent, what you need to look for to see if your child might have an eating disorder is if after eating a meal, the child leaves the room and goes into the bathroom or somewhere with a sink. This would indicate the child is binging (eating) and purging (throwing up). Or if the child just is playing with the food on their plate and does not eat very much, weight loss would become noticeable after a period of time and then they might have the sister disease anorexia.

Eating disorders are signs of serious psychological pain and are dangerous to your health and well being. Please don't suffer in silence. Get help. For bulimia and anorexia information on the Internet, visit www.ama.assn.org/ or www.healthlink.mcw.edu/article/901290364.html. If you don't yet have an eating disorder, but are interested in losing weight, write to:

Take off Pounds Sensibly Club
P.O. Box 07489
4575 South 5th Street
Milwaukee, WI 53207

Weight Watchers International
3860 Crenshaw Boulevard
Los Angeles, CA 90008.

If you are overweight and simply want support, write to:

Buxom Belles International
27856 Palomino Drive
Warren, MI 48093

National Association to Aid Fat Americans
P.O. Box 43
Bellerose, NY 11426.

Setting Goals

Setting goals is an area where a lot of people have trouble because they first of all have to know where to start. If you do not like to do a "project" alone, it is helpful to get a buddy to talk things over with and sometimes you can work better with someone. If you like to do things by yourself, but are not happy with the results, don't consider it a "failure." Use the experience to figure out what you need to do better or different next time.

For information and advice about setting goals, visit www.mindtools.com/page6 or www.innertalk.com on the Internet.

Information About Fraud

Fraud is the intentional misrepresentation of the truth in order to induce another person to part with something of value or surrender a legal right. Conviction for fraud requires proof that the victim relied on the misrepresentation to his detriment. A victim can sue to recover money that he or she lost as a result of fraud, but proving it can be difficult.

Proof of fraud requires that the person involved or buyer of a product relied on the intentional misrepresentation of a material fact. Suppose you take a tour of the basement, and see for yourself that the foundation is collapsing and that the cellar is full of water. You cannot later say that you relied on the owner's statement that the foundation was in top condition. Even if you did not see the damage, the fact that a reasonable and expected amount of diligence on your part would have disclosed it may be enough to invalidate a claim of fraud.

Americans are inundated by countless ads from radio and television, newspapers and mail. As a consequence, it is often difficult to tell the difference between ads that are truthful and ones that are false or misleading. Under federal and state laws, advertising that contains untrue statements is strictly prohibited. Omitting vital information can sometimes violate false-advertising laws, but the final cost will fall on the consumer who does not read the fine print or check all the things "included" in an ad.

The Federal Trade Commission is responsible for guarding against false advertising. Under federal law, an individual cannot file a civil lawsuit against a manufacturer for false advertising. However, the FTC can sue on behalf of consumers who have been harmed.

In recent years, the elderly have become the most frequent victims of scams. Scammers also use the Internet to try to defraud consumers and get their personal credit information. If you are the victim of a fraud, first notify the police and the sooner the better. If you were swindled by mail, inform your local postmaster so that an investigation can be initiated.

Social Security Fraud Hotline – Call toll free 1-800-269-0271

To get a discount on a book to help you protect yourself in hundreds of ways from scams and identity theft, go to www.aarp.org/books.
Securities and Exchange Commission
Federal Trade Commission
1-202-382-4357

If you were ever to be taken advantage of by Internet scams in what they called being phished there are free blocker tools called scamblockers.

Provided by Earthlink – free to all Internet users.

On the web: www.usps.com/postalinspectors
To stop postal fraud: call 1-877-987-3728
Get a free DVD called "Dialing for Dollars"
Hang up on phone fraud!

Sexual Harassment / Hostile Work Environment

If you are working in an atmosphere where there are any inappropriate remarks by any coworker or supervisor, take note. Watch for patterns and track the dates; record them and the times when the behavior happens.

If possible, start with the human resources department in your place of employment. Keep any written documents they may give you. This way, you will have documented proof of what's going on and it will aid you in stopping the behavior that's making you feel pressured or uncomfortable.

As I did, if you want assistance in your case, you should call a lawyer in your area that specializes in workplace harassment or misconduct. You can find them listed in your Yellow Pages.

The national addresses/phone numbers for your research and possible help are:

The US Department of Labor
Frances Perkins Building
200 Constitution Ave. NW
Washington, DC 20210

General Government Information, 1-800-688-9889. On the Internet, visit www.firstgov.gov

Problem Solving when Employment has been Terminated: Identifying the issues

Determine how much money is in your saving account.
Determine whether it is possible to borrow on your pension early.
Determine if there are cash values on your life insurance policies.
Find out your current amount of debt.
Call your bank and see if you can pay only the interest

on any current loans you may have.

Determine if you can refinance your mortgage at a lower rate.

Make a list of ways to save on current expenses.

See if you can find another position in the same company you were terminated from at a different location.

Check with your local unemployment office as soon as possible for immediate jobs available.

Determine if you should buy groceries in bulk to save on cost if you have storage room.

Before leaving make sure you get a letter of recommendation from your employer to help in your job search.

Domestic Violence and Child Abuse / Neglect

Statistics:

As many as seventy-three percent of the emergency room visits by battered women occur after separation from a violent partner/husband. (Stark and Flitcraft, 1981)

As many as seventy-five percent of calls made to police regarding domestic violence occur after separation. (U.S. Department of Justice, 1983)

Abuse of the battered woman and children may sharply escalate at the time parents separate, as the father attempts to reclaim the family or retaliate. (Bowker et al., 1988)

Forty children are abducted by a parent each hour in the United States. More than half of these abductions occur in the context of domestic violence. More than eighty percent of abductions by parents occur after separation. Almost forty percent of abductions by fathers involve force or violence. (Finklehor, et al, 1990; Greif and Hegar, 1992)

As much as ninety percent of the hostage taking in this country is domestic. Domestic hostage taking attempts to coerce a partner to return or remain in a marriage or relationship. One hundred percent of these hostage-takers are men. (F.B.I. 1989)

As many as fifty percent of women killed by partners/husbands are murdered at or after separation. (Wilson and Daly, 1991; Barnard, 1981)

During separation, women are five times more likely to be killed by their husbands than prior to separation or after divorce. (Crawford and Gartner, 1992)

Prepared by Barbara J. Hart, Esq., Pennsylvania Coalition Against Domestic Violence 1994. Reprinted with Permission.

Whether more children are abducted by strangers than in the past, or we simply hear more about it, is unclear. But one thing that has definitely changed since the 1960s is that strangers no longer have to meet children face-to-face to prey on them. With the advent of the Internet, children and teens spend a lot of time on the computer, sometimes in "chat rooms," where they can meet strangers who can hide behind false identities. Because the children think they are "chatting" with friends, not strangers, they may not sense when they are in danger of being exploited and won't tell a parent or other trusted adult.

If you notice changes in your child or any child you know, or if you have any other reason for alarm, even if it's just a hunch, please take your concerns seriously, as your actions could mean the difference between life and death. You must act as soon as you suspect anything.

Child abuse and neglect have been a problem throughout history in various forms, but have been brought to the forefront in recent history as a visible and important social problem. A humane approach to help both victims of child abuse and their families has developed (and is prominently expressed in the titles of various books on the subject), but a framework to involve lawmakers and the frontline medical practitioners still lags behind where it should be.

Education in schools about what parents should and should not do has come a long way since I was there. But when a child is dealing with abuse from a parent, we as a society are still deeply conflicted about the relation of children to the state, as well as to the family, and whether children have rights completely independent of their parents. Until the answer to this dilemma becomes clear, we shall never be able to enforce them.

Signs of abuse or neglect, such as bruises or changes in behavior, are seen if observed by educated individuals in a school setting, a hospital, the legal system, or in the neighborhood. These people can notice changes in the emotional makeup of the child or physical markings or injuries.

Under normal circumstances, parents have the right to custody of their children, the right to control and discipline them. Until someone outside the family reports suspected abuse or neglect, it will continue. Those who do report it can be granted immunity in the event that the report results in a criminal case. Do not worry about retaliation because your report will be kept confidential.

If you are being abused or are suffering in any way, do not feel ashamed or alone, as there are people out there who want to help you. I have been in your shoes and getting help can and will save your and your children's lives. The following are some resources you can access:

Domestic Violence Hotline: 1-800-799-7233

National Child Abuse and Neglect Hotline: 1-800- 422-4453

In desperate hours, for an understanding shoulder to lean on, call the National Suicide Hotline: 1-800-784-2433

Mental Health Hotline: 1-800-789-2647

Runaway National Hotline: 1-800-621-4000

Books that may help you include: *Relationship Rescue* or *Family First*, by Dr. Phil McGraw, PhD; and *The Control Freak*, by Les Parrott II, PhD.

To access a resource for parents of abused children, write to:
Parents Anonymous
22330 Hawthorne Boulevard, Suite 208
Torrance, CA 90505.

And for people who have been affected by sexual abuse, visit www.darkness2light.org, on the Internet.

www.bloomington.k12.mn.us/indschool/OLJ/Crisishelp – This is for abuse – either physical or sexual.

Addicted to pornography and/or sexual promiscuity? Go to www.freedomeveryday.org

SOME COMMON CHARACTERISTICS OF ABUSERS

There is no such thing as a "typical" abuser, but researchers have found that many:

FEEL A NEED FOR POWER AND CONTROL
– for some people, violence becomes a way to gain power and control. Because it works, the violence continues.

WITNESSED ABUSE AS CHILDREN
or were abused themselves. They see violence as a natural part of family life.

DON'T COMMUNICATE WELL
and have trouble expressing their true feelings.

HAVE A POOR SELF-IMAGE
and feel unable to control their lives. Abuse may be a violent attempt to show control.

ABUSE ALCOHOL
or other drugs. This habit may be used as an excuse – "I was drunk, I didn't know what I was doing." It may also loosen a person's self-control.

ARE AFRAID OF ABANDONMENT
Many abusers are tortured by thoughts of losing their partner.

FEEL INTENSE JEALOUSY
This often arises from low self-esteem.

Some men abuse simply because they think they can. They may not respect the fact that abuse is a crime!

Handout given at a conference by the Coalition for Domestic Violence.

American Legal System

I have gained experience in the American legal system, though not by choice. Knowledge is power, goes the old saying, and that is so true in the field of law. If you are armed with the right facts, you can avoid legal pitfalls, bail yourself out of trouble, minimize potential losses, become a smarter consumer, and take full advantage of the rights and benefits you are entitled to as a citizen of the United States. But even though the American legal system is for the protection of all US citizens, I will always call it the criminal justice system, as in "justice for criminals."

I have gone through the American legal system and, while this guide is not intended to be a substitute for a lawyer, it can serve as a trusted adviser for the basic information to help you understand the legal system and get you started on the right track. Without a doubt, in some situations you know yourself, you will need to call a lawyer right away to avoid serious consequences. Hopefully, if you follow the laws of the land, you will not need to go to court. But if you break the law, the following basic layout of how it works may be helpful.

State courts are organized in levels. Almost all have three levels: the lowest, where cases are tried; the middle, where cases are appealed; and the highest, where cases are further appealed. In some states, they do not have the middle level and go right to the top.

A trial court will hear the evidence, decide the facts of the case, and apply the law to those facts. Depending on the local custom, trial courts may be called district court, circuit court, superior court, county court or courts of common pleas. At this level, they have what is called "general jurisdiction," which means they hear all types of cases. They can range from specialties such as probate court (wills, estates, property) and juvenile/family court, to municipal court, whose cases involve limited amounts of money (small claims), traffic court, and magistrates' court. The whole system is designed to settle disputes. Sometimes they are between two citizens and sometimes, when they are serious matters, the state takes over and it becomes the state versus the citizen.

Sooner or later in life, you will probably need a lawyer to advise you about a problem or to settle a dispute. But you may not know if your situation needs one. In general, you should consult a lawyer if your problem is complex, if it involves a lot of money, or if the consequences of not doing so could be severe.

Waiting until a problem arises before finding a lawyer may mean that you choose one under extreme stress. This may be very costly to you, not only financially, but in that you might not get the best lawyer for your type of case or situation. It's always good to listen to people you know and keep in mind the name of a lawyer someone has used so you will know whom to call when a crisis hits.

If you have the time to "shop" for a lawyer for a specific type of situation, you need to get organized to find a suitable one. Many attorneys offer a free or low-cost first consultation. Ask about this, as well as any fees for other services at the time that you schedule an interview. The goal you should have in mind is to assess the lawyer's competence and determine whether your personalities are compatible. You must "make a good fit" because under stress, you must have complete trust in them.

Prison Families Anonymous
353 Fulton Avenue
Hempstead, NY 11550
For families of prisoners

For many legal problems, you can take care of them yourself without the need of a lawyer. Some of the things you can take care of are separations, real estate matters, prenuptial agreements, bankruptcy and divorce. This can be done with the right forms that you can fill out yourself and then just have them notarized. To get the forms, some of them are FREE, go to these web sites:

www.freeforms.com or www.uslegalforms.com

Alcohol and Drug Abuse

Sometimes the crutches we use to cope with traumatic situations add their own stress. In my life, one such coping mechanism was alcohol consumption. My first experience trying alcohol on my own was at the age thirteen. My mother had a bottle of whiskey in the kitchen cabinet and I was emotionally upset about something. I don't recall what it was, whether boy troubles or peer pressure; but I was curious, too. I also had a lot of insecurity in my life. My mother was very ill most of the time and since my father had died a few years before, I never knew when "the next shoe would fall." The drink relaxed me and that felt good. But it wasn't actually a good thing for me because it introduced me to the realization that alcohol could help me temporarily forget my emotional feelings.

During the 1970s, drugs were everywhere. If you wanted anything, you could get it. I wasn't interested, but most of my friends were trying pot and assorted things. I was afraid of it and thought only "bad people" did that stuff. After a couple of years of being around it, though, I was curious enough that I felt like trying some of it. My excuse was that I would be able to speak from experience about whether it was good or bad and I would have the "authority" to make my opinion valid.

Whenever there was alcohol at parties, I drank to excess, as I did not know how to stop before I had too much. I guess I was a binge social drinker, but I never let it affect my schoolwork or home life. I was a good kid in all respects — I graduated high school and college and got married. I had two sons and continued to be just a social drinker.

One of the first and most important things to remember is that any substance you take into your body is something that your body has to process. If it's natural and has nutrients, then your system will benefit from it. Alcohol and marijuana (pot) are two very common substances used by people of all ages today. At one time, alcohol was illegal and that time period was called prohibition. Today, millions are fighting to get pot legalized for medical use. But use of these and other substances like methamphetamines (speed), LSD, cocaine, and other various street drugs is not only illegal, but can be deadly the first time you or anyone you know tries them. If alcohol or drugs are used in excess or for an extended period of time, the abuse becomes addictive and controls the person and his life.

Abuse reasons usually stem from a root cause, such as a disconnect in emotional development as the young person is growing up. I now see that was the case for my alcohol abuse — my need for security in my youth and then alcohol blurred my reality.

What you must first work on if you are abusing a substance or you care about someone who is, is to get to the core of what is creating the need to use. Second, support is of utmost importance! Don't tell the person you are trying to help what not to do. Give them things and options of what they can do. Give positive reinforcements, not negative.

The following are places where you can get information in your search for help:

Alcoholics Anonymous
AA World Services
P.O. Box 459
Grand Central Station
New York, NY 10163

Al-Anon Family
Group Headquarters
One Park Avenue
New York, NY 10016

Families in Action (for parents concerned about drug abuse)
3845 North Druid Hills Rd., Suite 300
Decatur, GA 30030

National Assoc. on Drug Abuse
355 Lexington Avenue
New York, NY 10017

Alcohol Prevention and Treatment National Hotline, 1-800-729-6686; and on the Internet, you can find many helpful sites by searching for "Alcoholics Anonymous" or "drug addiction." You can also visit www.overcomersoutreach.org or www.stopalcoholabuse.gov.

www.abovetheinfluence.com

Forgiveness

Resources for learning to make forgiveness a part of your life include: www.turningpoint.org and www.tbn. org or 1-800-637-2228 and 1-614-837-3232.

Depression

Order a free depression evaluation kit off the Internet from www.lifeiswaiting.com. For a free tape called *Count Your Blessings*, go to www.awmi.net, and get a free compact disc by visiting www.cfaith.com. You can also visit www.depressionhurts.com.

Call about Faith at 1-800-748-8107 and call Breakthrough at 1-800-365-8055

Former patients with mental disorders, such as depression and other emotional problems, may write to:
Recovery, Inc.
116 South Michigan Ave.
Chicago, IL 60603.

Good Choices and Avoiding Stress
Some resources to help you make right choices or to get answers to your questions regarding this topic include: 1-800-727-9673; Paula White at 1-800-874-7729; and www.joycemeyer.org.

Find Your Purpose in Life
To start on your path to finding your purpose in life, call 1-877-768-1999. Read a Bible or parts of one. On the web you can visit www.edyoung.org, www.changinglives.org, or www.answersbc.org or read the book *The Purpose Driven Life* by Rick Warren. It can be

found at your local bookstore or on the web at www. PurposeDrivenLife.com. Visit a local church.

Your Responsibility to America

I beg you to search your own soul and put into action what your convictions are to help America toward a good and brighter future.

TBN toll-free at 1-888-731-1000 and Breakthrough at 1-800-365-8055. For up-to-the-minute updates on what is happening and what you can do concerning the turmoil in Israel visit the web site www.watch.org.

Contact Your Government
On the web
reclaimingamerica.org

Ladies Auxilliary
Military Order of the Purple Heart
419 Franklin Street
Reading, MA 01867
For wives of soldiers who have been wounded

The Center for Moral Clarity
Issues and Legislation

The bible was removed from our school systems in 1963.
To have the bible put back and used as a source of literature and a historical document, which it is. Call toll free 1-888-BIBLE-NOW

To learn the complete details of our founding fathers personal religious beliefs who felt that prayer and the bible should be in schools, go to the web site www.wallbuilders.com.

155

Over 35 states have passed the bill that says the bible needs to be included in our schools as a true source of history and literature. To find out what curriculum should be taught in our school systems today, go to the web site www. bibleinschools.net.

Post-Traumatic Stress Disorder

I will explain just what post-traumatic stress disorder is. It's common for people to feel that no matter what they've faced or lived with, no matter how extreme, they should be able to carry on. But sometimes people face situations that are so traumatic that they become unable to cope and function in their daily lives. The extreme trauma that can cause this reaction could be a terrifying event or ordeal that the person has experienced, witnessed or learned about, especially one that's life threatening or causes physical harm. It can be a single event or a repeated experience. The experience causes the person to feel intense fear, horror or a sense of helplessness and the stress caused by the trauma can affect all aspects of the person's life, including mental, emotional, and physical well being.

Some people become so distressed by memories of the trauma — memories that won't go away — that they begin to live their lives trying to avoid any reminders of what happened to them. A person who still feels this way, months after a traumatic experience has passed, may be suffering from post-traumatic stress disorder (PTSD), a serious and common health condition. And research suggests that prolonged trauma may disrupt and alter brain chemistry. For some people, this may lead to the development of PTSD if they had not previously been diagnosed with it. For these people, getting beyond the trauma and overcoming it requires professional help.

Posttraumatic Stress Disorder (PTSD) – AACAP Facts
For Families #70
www.aacap.org/publications/factsfam/ptsd70.htm

WebMD: Post-Traumatic Stress Disorder Topic Over-
view
my.webmd.com/hw/mental_health/hw184190.asp

PTSD
www.ptsdalliance.org/home2.html

Post Traumatic Stress Disorder
www.burnsurvivorsttw.org/articles/ptsd.html

NIMH: Post-Traumatic Stress Disorder (PTSD)
www.nimh.nih.gov/HealthInformation/ptsdmenu.cfm

HealthyMinds.org – Healthy minds. Healthy lives.
www.Healthyminds.org

National Center for PTSD // National Center for Post-
Traumatic Stress Disorder
www.ncptsd.va.gov/

Anxiety Disorders – Post Traumatic Stress Disorder
www.nmha.org/reassurance/ptsd.cfm

Posttraumatic Stress Disorder
www.mentalhealth.com/dis/p20-an06.html

Statistics:

An estimated seventy percent of adults in the United
States have experienced a traumatic event at least once in
their lives, and up to twenty percent of these people go on
to develop PTSD.

An estimated five percent of Americans — more than thirteen million people — have PTSD at any given time.

Approximately eight percent of all adults — one of thirteen people in this country — will develop PTSD during their life.

Women are about twice as likely to get PTSD than men, since women tend to experience interpersonal violence (such as domestic violence, rape or abuse) more often than men.

Almost seventeen percent of men and thirteen percent of women have experienced more than three traumatic events in their lives.

The estimated risk for developing PTSD for people who have experienced the following traumatic events is:

Rape (49%)

Severe beating or assault (31.9%)

Other sexual assault (23.7%)

Serious accident or injury; for example, car, train, or other type accident (16.8%)

Shooting or stabbing (15.4%)

Sudden, unexpected death of a family member or friend (14.3%)

Child's life-threatening illness (10.4%)

Witness to killing or serious injury (7.3%)

Natural disaster (3.8%)

Given the September 11 terrorist attacks that affected so many people, the occurrence of PTSD has risen dramatically and the war in Iraq is increasing the numbers. There is more information available to you on the web at WWW. PTSDALLIANCE.COM/RESOURCES.HTML. They have free information about books and guides on post-traumatic stress disorder.

Surgery

If you face any type of surgery, whether medically necessary, elective reconstructive or cosmetic, please consider these points:

What you do will always have some risk attached to it. Any time you have an invasive procedure done to your body, you risk infection, healing problems or disappointment over the outcome of a cosmetic procedure that doesn't meet your expectations.

If you are having cosmetic surgery, make sure you prepare yourself mentally for the real issue of why. "Beauty is only skin deep" is a saying that has its basis in truth. You must have good self-esteem first, and then go ahead with a procedure in the hope that its results will meet with what you feel inside is the real you.

Having had many spinal injuries myself, I've found that spinal cord injury is very common. And since spinal cord damage is one of the most serious injuries a person can have, and millions of people have problems with their spines/backs, I feel it helpful to include information about it.

Any damage to the spinal cord is a complex injury. People who are injured are often confused when trying to understand what it means to be a person with a spinal cord injury (SCI). This is a brief explanation of the spine, how it works, and how an injury can affect a person.

The Normal Spinal Cord

The spinal cord is a part of your nervous system and is the largest nerve in your body. Nerves are cord-like structures made up of many nerve fibers. The spinal cord has many spinal nerve fibers that carry messages between the brain and different parts of the body. The messages may tell a body part to move. Other nerve fibers send and receive messages of feeling or sensation back to the brain from the body, such as heat, cold, or pain. The body has an autonomic nervous system. This means it controls the involuntary activities of the body, such as blood pressure, body temperature, and sweating. The spinal cord and nerve fibers can be compared to a telephone system. The telephone cable (spinal cord) sends messages to and from a main office (the brain) to individual offices (body parts).

Because the spinal cord is such an important part of our nervous system, it is surrounded and protected by bones. These are called vertebrae, or backbones, and are stacked on top of each other. The bones have cushions between them called discs. This system of bones is called the spinal column and the spinal cord runs through the middle of the vertebrae. The column is about eighteen inches long. It goes from the base of the brain, down the middle of the back, to about the waist. The nerves that branch off the spinal cord do so between the vertebrae and go out to all parts of the body. At the end of the spinal cord, the lower spinal fibers continue down through the spinal canal to the sacrum, or tailbone.

Damage or Injury to the Spinal Cord

Damage to the spinal cord can occur from either a traumatic injury or from a disease to the vertebral column. In most spinal injuries, the backbone or a disc pinches the cord, causing it to become bruised or swollen. Sometimes the injury may tear the cord and/or its nerve fibers. When this happens, from the point of injury and below it, the spinal cord nerves cannot send messages between the brain and parts of the body, as they did before the injury or disease.

In 1995, actor Christopher Reeve sustained a broken neck that severed his spinal cord at that level and left him unable to move from the neck down. It was his determination and drive to work not only to improve his own life, but also the lives of others with spinal cord injuries, that brought SCI to the forefront of peoples' minds.

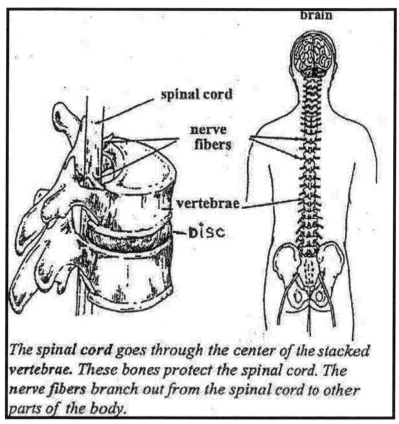

The spinal cord goes through the center of the stacked vertebrae. These bones protect the spinal cord. The nerve fibers branch out from the spinal cord to other parts of the body.

From a handout given out by the Medical College of Virginia
Harold F. Young Neurosurgical Center

Following is a large list of important addresses, web sites, and toll-free numbers you can use to get information on the subject of spinal cord injury.

Christopher & Dana Reeve Paralysis Resource Center
800-539-7309
email: info@paralysis.org
www.paralysis.org

Provides a comprehensive, national source of information for people living with paralysis. You may email questions or call the toll-free number to speak with an Information Specialist.

National Spinal Cord Injury Assoc (NSCIA)
800-962-9629 or 301-588-6959
email: nscia2@aol.com
www.spinalcord.org
6701 Democracy Blvd, Ste 300-9,
Bethesda, MD 20817

The NSCIA works to develop programs and services and act as community advocates for individuals with SCI, families, and health care providers. They support and encourage research aimed at improving care for persons with SCI and developing a cure for spinal cord injury and disease.

Online Communication Resources
Through the Internet and Communication Software you can "talk" to others via your computer. Connect to news groups, bulletin boards, discussion groups, message boards, and Chat Rooms for topics related to SCI and disabilities.

Canadian Abilities Foundation
www.enablelink.org/chat.html?showchat=1

Disabled Individuals Movement for Equality Network (DIMENET)
www.dimenet.com

ICan.com
www.ican.com/board/forum.cfm

KWNPF Bulletin Board
www.spinalvictory.org/community/forum/

New Mobility Magazine Chat Room
www.newmobility.com/chat/cfm
Quad-link

www.2tim.net
Quad-list
http://come.to/quadlist

Vent-Users Discussion Group
www.eskimo.com/~jlubin/disabled/ventuser.htm

Magazines & Newsletters

Disability Resources Monthly
516-585-0290
Email: info@disabilityresources.org
www.disabilityresources.org/DRMpubs-DRM.html
Subscription: $30 (US) 1 year
Four Glatter Lane, Centereach, NY 11720-1032
This newsletter features articles, reviews, and news about free, inexpensive, and hard-to-find books, pamphlets, videotapes, online sources, and organizations.

Inter@ct
408-295-9896
www.tbi-sci.org
This bi-annual newsletter of the Santa Clara Valley Medical Center's Rehabilitation Research Center on traumatic brain injury and spinal cord injury, reports news in both areas from this Center. Also available via email.

New Mobility Magazine
888-850-0344
Email: info@newmobility.com
www.newmobility.com
Subscription: $27.95 (US) 1 year
P.O. Box 220, Horsham, PA 19044
Publisher of magazine and books on disability issues, especially spinal cord injury.

Paraplegia News
888-888-2201
Email: pvapub@aol.com
www.pn-magazine.com
Subscription: $23 (US) 1 year
2111 E. Highland Ave, Ste 180,
Phoenix, AZ 85016-4702
This magazine, published by the PVA, covers the latest on spinal-cord-injury research, new products, legislation, people with disabilities, accessible travel, computers, and more. PVA also publishes Sports 'n Spokes magazine.

Pushin' On
205-934-3283
Email: rtc@uab.edu
www.spinalcord.uab.edu/show.asp?durki=21396
Subscription: Free to individuals with SCI
UAB RRTC in SCI, 619 19th St. S, SRC 529,
Birmingham, AL 35249-7330
Newsletter published twice a year covering health, research, and other issues related to secondary conditions of SCI.

The Project
305-243-6001
Email: mpinfo@miamiproject.med.miami.edu
www.themiamiproject.miami.edu.newsltr.htm
Subscription: Free online
P.O. Box 016960 (R-48), Miami, Florida 33101-6960
Newsletter published 3 times a year about work of the Miami Project to Cure Paralysis.

SCI Access
734-936-4000
Email: model_sci@umich.edu
www.med.umich.edu/pmr/model_sci/newsletter.htm
Subscription: Free online
Newsletter of the Univ Michigan-Model SCI System,

providing information on living effectively with SCI to persons with SCI, family members, and interested parties. Published 2 times/year.

Spinal Cord Injury Update
206-685-3999
Email: rehab@u.washington.edu
http://depts.washington.edu/rehab/sci/update.shtml
Issues: 4 issues per year
Box 356490, Seattle, Washington 98195-6490
Newsletter by Univ of Washington, Rehabilitation Medicine that contains articles on SCI for health care providers and consumers, as well as summaries of current literature on SCI.

Paralyzed Veterans of America
801 18th St NW, Washington, DC 20006
800-424-8200
Email: info@pva.org
www.pva.org

RRTC on Aging with Spinal Cord Injury
Rancho Los Amigos Medical Center
7601 E Imperial Hwy, 800 West Annex
Downey, CA 90242-3456
562-401-7402
www.agingwithsci.org

Web address is www.abms.com

Here are a couple more addresses to help you with your current needs when facing physical challenges.

Society for the Rehabilitation of the Facially Disfigured
550 First Avenue
New York, NY 1001
For persons with facial disfigurement and their families.

National Association of the Physically Handicapped
76 Elm Street
London, Ohio 43140
For physically handicapped persons and their families needing assistance.

Head Injury

Emotional support from family and friends is critical to recovery. The amount of healing and recovery depends on the type of damage or brain injury. The outcome will depend on what treatment was given and by no means does the impression of how bad it seems when the first injury occurs suggest a gloomy outlook for the future. However, it is not only the patient who will need support. Families and other loved ones will also need support and compassion as they learn to live with the brain injured person, whose personality may have changed and who may be prone to emotional outbursts or other erratic behavior.

It will come as no surprise that, as a result of my experiences, I have learned a lot about head and brain injury. I will try to explain the ways in which the brain may be damaged in an accident and the effects of this damage. You should remember that I am describing a wide range of possibilities and that you or the person you are concerned about may have been affected in only one or two of the ways I describe. If you are in doubt about anything, or if what I say worries you, talk it over with a doctor or the doctor who has been your contact at the hospital or clinic.

Three Types of Head Injury

Closed
A closed head injury is called this because there is usu-

ally no break in the skin or an open wound. This can happen when the head suddenly changes its motion. Examples include a sudden stop when a car runs into a tree or brick wall (deceleration) or when one car is hit from behind at a traffic light (acceleration). Another example is a sudden head roll from a knockout punch to the jaw (rotation).

This is the injury most of you know as a concussion. As these movements happen, the brain is forced to follow the movement of the skull. Since the brain is soft and jelly-like, it can get twisted and distorted in the process. This is when the millions of nerve fibers are stretched and damaged. The arteries and veins that run through the brain can be torn, causing blood to leak from them, making a bruise that is very like one you can get anywhere else on you body, such as a bump on your arm. Because there is room for the brain to move inside the skull, it slides on the inner surface of the bone. This surface has raised edges and sharp ridges that can further bruise and damage the brain's surface.

Some of the most damaging closed head injuries occur when a person suffers a stroke. This is when blood is cut off to the brain due to a blood clot or bleeding in the brain. Also, blood can be cut off to the brain due to a heart attack or drowning. The longer the brain goes without blood, the more brain cells will die. It also depends on which parts of the brain are cut off from blood flow. This will determine what type of damage the brain incurs and thus, what type of long-term effects the person will have.

Penetrating

In a penetrating head injury, the scalp is cut through, the bone of the skull beneath it can be broken up, and the brain may be exposed and damaged. Some causes of this type of injury include a collision with a sharp object, such as a broken steering wheel, and being hit by a bullet. The open injury, unfortunately, is often accompanied by an acceleration type injury as well. If this is not the case, however, the brain area away from the immediate area of the injury is likely to be undamaged. In the long term, there may be very little disability in spite of what seems at the time to be a frightening injury.

Crushing

In a crushing head injury, the head may be caught between a boat and a wharf or under the wheel of a car. Thankfully, this is the least common type of injury.

Visible and Hidden Effects —
How the Brain Functions After Injury

The above types of head injuries happen in a matter of seconds and are what is called the "first injury." The "second injury" is what happens during the time following what caused the first. Understanding the chain of events has led to great improvements in the way rescue squads and trauma teams operate. The first thing they must do is make sure the patient is breathing so the oxygen supply to the brain is good and the blood pressure gets back to normal. By doing this, the trip to the hospital is safer and further injury to the brain from lack of oxygen can be prevented.

The "third injury" is what happens next and can happen any time after the first two. Usually, it's during the next two to three days, but can be up to months later. When the brain is bruised on first impact, it reacts the same way as the body does — it swells because fluid leaks out into it. However, the effect in the head is much more important than in other parts of the body. When the brain swells, if the skull isn't broken, the brain has no room to expand and so will suffer more damage. If the pressure is not lowered, the brain will die.

Also of great concern are blood clots. When bruising occurs during the first injury, small veins and arteries are torn and this results in blood leakage. This is common and can occur in very minor injuries, so even they must be taken seriously.

For more information, consult *Head Injury, The Facts: A Guide for Families and Caregivers*, by Dorothy Gronwall, Philip Wrightson, and Peter Waddell. You can also use the Internet to check your local brain injury support groups or visit www.tbichat.org. I found this site to be the most helpful for information and especially for personal support.

Association for Children with Retarded Mental Development
817 Broadway
New York, NY 10030
For parents of children with brain injury also caused by birth trauma

Brain Injury Association of America
www.biausa.org/

The Brain Trauma Foundation
www.braintrauma.org/

Brain Injury Resource Center
www.headinjury.com/

I entered the following poem in the Ahead of the Times Poetry Contest, sponsored by the Traumatic Brain Injury Web Site www.tbichat.org.

Mary Ann Worsham

OUR DREAMS AND STRUGGLES IN THE TRAUMATIC BRAIN INJURY "CLUB"

Original poem by Mary Ann Worsham

We've come to know each other here in this club not
knowing we would be so glad,
because in the past life seemed to be fine,
until we were suddenly sad.
Sad we lost the person who "was" and
sad our dreams had to change,
but with adjustments, determination and hope in
our hearts new goals are within our range.
So as a member of the TBI club we share our feelings and love,
and realize that we are here and OK
by the grace of the good lord above.
The choice we made to pursue our dreams came
out of our struggles and needs,
it was not easy but they survived like
small little seeds.
Through years of pain, effort and care,
we work for the day that we will be "there".
With our TBI we have come to the place we can start,
using our talents, our skills and our heart.
I wish for myself and for all of you too,
that we all will be happy in whatever we do.
So from this day on until our last,
Look towards the future but remember the past.
Life is ahead and that is the test,
Good luck to you all, I WISH YOU THE BEST!

Step / Blended Families

Remarriages have been common in the United States since the country's beginnings, but until the last century, almost all remarriages followed widowhood. In the Plymouth Colony, for instance, about one-third of all men and one-quarter of all women lived full lifetimes remarried after the death of a spouse, but there was little divorce. Even as late as the 1920s, more brides and grooms were remarrying after widowhood than after divorce, according to most estimates.

In 1900, only about three percent of brides and grooms were divorced. In 1930, the incidence was about nine percent. By 1975, it was estimated that it had grown to approximately twenty-five percent. Most of the rise has been the result of the increase in the divorce rate. The rate of divorce for marriages that occur now is at about sixty percent.

Can these marriages after divorce, many of which include children from previous marriages, maintain unity as well as do families of first marriages? A number of studies have shown a greater risk of separation and divorce for remarriages after divorce. Remarriage after widowhood, in contrast, is much less. Divorce happens less as a person who loses a spouse usually does not have any "bad baggage" to take with them into a new marriage.

One explanation is that the problems of remarried people arise from personality issues that preceded their marriages. People in troubled marriages have unresolved personal conflicts that must be faced and worked on before a successful marriage can be achieved. Their problems lead them to marry second or third spouses who may be superficially quite different from their first spouses, but are really quite similar. As a result, this causes remarried people to repeat the problems of their first marriages.

Other possible reasons include a person being less will-

171

ing to repeat mistakes, so she expects more from the new spouse and puts unrealistic expectations on him. This can cause extreme stress, but with effort, can be resolved. Some remarried men are deficient at fulfilling their economic responsibilities because they need to support a previous set of children and new ones in the new marriage. But the blame cannot be placed only on men, as women today are breadwinners in greater numbers than they have been in the past, so financial burdens can be spread between the two adults.

The question of how to fairly treat the children, whether from each spouse's previous marriage or the current one, is also a challenge. The children from previous marriages are usually in the custody of the mother, but they normally visit the non-custodial parent (father) regularly. Thus, there must be good communication among all parties involved. If this is not happening, abuse occurs and the children become pawns in a power struggle. If you are considering remarriage, I recommend that you discuss with your future spouse all the important things that you want in a relationship and how every family member will be treated.

One thing to think about is planning for division of property if your marriage should fail. This is called a prenuptial agreement. But again, you must discuss all issues about what you want out of your relationship so you have the best chance for it to work. If you don't do this beforehand, you will be in for a rude surprise. You may be more likely to bail out of a second marriage since you have gone through one divorce and will feel it's easier to leave the next time when things get "rough."

There are many books on the market, but one that I highly recommend is *Family First*, by Dr. Phil McGraw.

Aging Parents

Hopefully, your parents will be in good health and able to plan their own affairs for when they retire. I will give you advice and information to assist you in getting things arranged the way they want them to be and the best way for you to handle them if you are responsible for them.

Too many Americans find themselves approaching retirement with inadequate financial security. With no pension or individual retirement account to provide them with income, they rely on payments from Social Security. But Social Security benefits were not meant to cover all retirement needs, and retirees should not count on them exclusively. Begin to plan for your later years early in your working life — the earlier the better. Federal laws allow employers to establish 401(K) tax-deferred savings plans, pension plans, and IRAs for their employees. The self-employed can set up plans that allow them to build up tax-deferred savings too.

To avoid delays if you're going to apply for your Social Security benefits and to make sure you receive what benefits you are entitled to, make sure your Social Security records are up to date. If you disagree with any assessment of your benefits, you must file an appeal in writing. This must be done within sixty days of the time you receive the first notification about your benefits. As a last resort, you can hire a lawyer and take matters into your own hands.

One of the most important issues with aging parents is how the family will deal with the changing roles of each family member. Differences in age mean differences in life stage concerns and experiences, which, for example, are reflected in considerations of life space. The male in our society is often portrayed as overburdened with commitments to family, work and community. The female is busy with raising the children and, now, also working outside the home. So many are caught in a "life cycle squeeze," commonly called The Sandwich Generation.

The process of aging, itself, has changed over time. The ages at which roles are assumed or relinquished, health and income status, and self-definitions are ever evolving. When is one "old," what is it to be old, how does one behave as an older person? Members of different families will answer these questions differently, largely as consequences of the families' experiences and current situations.

If parent-child interaction in later life resembles more the process of friendship than that of earlier intra-family relations, relying upon similarities of values and attitudes, then the family should be able to operate in an agreeable and attractive way between the generations. Aging parents will not have to make demands upon their children if they have planned well for their retirement, although many may do so. Adult children will be spared excruciating choices between the needs of their own children, themselves, and their parents.

Those bonds that do endure will do so because they have been willingly sought and nurtured by adults who are authentically concerned with one another's well being. Far from disintegrating, the future of parent-child relations in later life may be characterized by the strongest ties of all, mutual respect.

Toll-free information: Aging (Parents) Information Hotline, 1-800-677-1116; General Government Information, 1-800-688-9889; and for long-term care information, 1-800-PLAN-LTC.

You can also write to:

US Administration on Aging
Health and Human Services
200 Independence Ave. SW
Washington, DC 20201

Gray Panthers (an activist senior citizens organization)
3700 Chestnut Street
Philadelphia, PA 19104

On the Internet, visit the National Institute on Aging's web site at www.nia.nih.gov. For info on caregivers' and workers' rights, go to www.dol.gov and click on Family and Medical Leave Act.

Funeral History and Planning

The art of funeral directing as it is practiced today in the United States is considered to be relatively new and different, although the history of caring for the dead can be traced back as far as the first recorded history of man. The Greek and Roman civilizations were very similar. It is clearly deduced from history that they adhered to the belief that disembodied spirits haunted the living by wandering about their households.

In Egypt, the care of the dead was well organized. Emphasis was placed on the embalming of the dead body by the embalmer priests. Egyptians placed great pride on leaving with the body of the deceased treasured things that they had loved or owned in life, as it was believed that they would be of great help to them in the afterlife. They also had tremendous investments in the coffins, such as you see for the pharaohs such as King Tut.

The early Christians conducted services in secret. They used underground chambers known as catacombs, such as those found underneath Rome. In Europe during the medieval period, up to AD 1700, the first evidence of their fancy coffins appeared. The bodies of people of high rank were placed in heavy oak or lead coffins. The families and the clergy were in charge of the disposition of the dead person.

In the United States, most of the early funeral customs were introduced from England. The early American undertaker, in the period up to the Civil War, did very little in the way of embalming. The modern concept of funeral homes was totally unknown. An undertaker usually was the village carpenter or liveryman, since his work consisted of making coffins and of furnishing carriages for the funeral procession.

Funerals were largely held in the home of the deceased until the twentieth century. Preservation was provided in most instances prior to AD 1880 by means of ice chests, which were wooden boxes provided with trays for the body and compartments to receive the ice. The upper part of the chest had a window in it, through which the body could be viewed. With the Civil War and thousands of families wanting their loved ones to be sent home, it was necessary for embalming techniques to evolve into what we know today.

Modern funeral service has evolved through the ages as a specialized, highly skilled care-taking profession. Mortuary arts and sciences today embrace all the functions incident to death and burial ceremonies. The bereaved family can better adjust to life following the loss of a family member by having a funeral service for the deceased. The funeral is the basis for the acceptance of death, affirming the dignity of the deceased to provide for the expression of emotion and for comfort for the family.

The Foundation and Reasons for Funeral Services

Psychological

The individual psychological needs of the family are met by having a funeral for the family member who has died. The needs are met in the following ways: the funeral allows for the normal expression of emotion through crying; there is freedom to verbalize feelings; friends and family provide support; the service helps emphasize death's reality; the ceremony provides spiritual support; the funeral service provides comfort; it allows a person to begin the grieving process and deal with any feelings they may have in a healthy way; viewing of the dead human remains helps to establish the realization of the finality of death.

Religious
Since the mortician is a public servant, he or she must serve people of all religions. Religious rituals have marked influence upon customs and procedure of conduct and are very slow to change. The symbolism and ideology of the three great religious groups, Protestant, Roman Catholic, and Jewish, need to be understood to serve these people satisfactorily. Other faiths are quite varied in customs and are essentially adapted from the major religious groups. Since the beginning of time, all funeral rites were carried out with a religious or superstitious significance.

Racial
Each racial group, because of certain inherent traditions that have evolved through the ages, has developed certain customs, which are adhered to today in greater or lesser degree. The mounding of graves, construction of tombs, cave burials, cremation, wakes, watchers, mourning habits, self-chastisement, etc., are practices that are evident in modern funeral service in a modified form.

Social
Each funeral service is of social significance in several ways. As part of society, the individual actually or potentially contributes to the whole order. Death removes the person physically, spiritually, and mentally, causing a marked change in the social pattern of which he or she was a part. Those elements and people affected by the loss react to the situation in varied ways. This will greatly influence the way in which people carry out their funeral arrangements, from the discrete to the ostentatious.

Economic

The family's material wealth is very often a controlling factor in the funeral service. The expenditure of money when considering arrangements directly affects the economic situation of the dependents. The loss of income, loss of potential and actual services to society, and change of life pattern of dependents all have a bearing on the procedure followed in the burial of the individuals.

Sentimental

The first reaction to death is a sentimental one. Loss of a loved one removes the physical being and personality of that individual around whom society has built up a character based on love, honor, devotion, and respect. The reaction of family and friends to this death are reflected in the way the funeral service will be planned. The arrangements made are a direct reflection of the sentimental aspect of the death, varying from simple to very elaborate ceremonies. Customs that are traditional in funeral rites have evolved through the years, but change has been very slow and sentiment has been one of the biggest influences on decision making.

What You Need to Know to Prepare for What We Will All Go Through

Funeral service is both a profession and a business. Since the funeral practitioner offers both service and merchandise, he/she is considered a professional and a businessperson. The funeral director must be aware of the various characteristics that are necessary for servicing people during times of emotional distress. These include courtesy, sympathy, understanding, even temperament, pleasing personality, sincerity, dignity, and honesty.

You must know that funeral professionals have the utmost respect for handling the deceased. Removal of the person from where they died is done with great care. The body is properly covered at all times and care is taken to see that at no time is the body ever left uncovered. Even when the body is in the preparation room, it is always covered when not being worked on. I had a family ask me to put the man's favorite pajamas on him for the night that he spent in the funeral home before the visitation, and to leave a light on because he didn't like to be in a dark room. I did as they asked.

Arrangements
Before the family comes to the funeral home to make arrangements, they are told to bring with them the necessary papers, such as all aspects of the deceased's vital statistics information used for the death certificate. The next of kin must also give the funeral director permission to embalm the body. Some individuals and families prefer cremation, so that decision is told to the director at that time. If the family chooses embalming, they are told to bring with them any special cosmetics the person liked, special clothing the person had chosen or family would like for them to wear, and the name of a hairdresser if a special one is wanted, although all funeral homes provide that service for the family.

By law, the first thing discussed when the family arrives is a disclosure of written materials showing the family all of the prices that could be incurred by what the family chooses during the upcoming arrangement time.

Next, the family history is taken and used to write up an obituary if the family wants to put one in the newspaper. Then a review of available death benefits the family is entitled to occurs. These could include Social Security benefits, veteran's benefits, railroad retirement benefits, proceeds from life insurance policies or burial or pre-need insurance, or benefits from a lodge or union.

An explanation of the usual number of pallbearers (casket carriers) would be given next. It is usually six or eight. The family may then want to discuss who they would like

179

to perform the funeral service and at what place, whether at a church, the funeral home or some other site. Musical selections can be chosen and other personal touches for the service are decided at this time. Next, the family would be taken into the casket selection room to see what type of casket they would like to place their loved one in. This can be very distressing for them.

Many other details are discussed during arrangements and phone calls may be made between the time of the initial consultation and when the family has decided to have the first visitation.

Take it from me, it's better to have a living will and a regular will. It really helped me that Richard and I had them drawn up two weeks before my attack. Also, prearrange your funeral and you will save your family a tremendous amount of stress and grief when the time actually comes.

And while this is something that will have occurred before you get to the funeral home, I'll include it here. When you're planning ahead, also give serious consideration to organ and tissue donation. It will save your family the concern of making this sometimes difficult decision and, if you decide in favor of it, you will contribute greatly to another family's happiness. Visit www.donatelife.net or www.save7lives.org for more information.

For more information and free forms to help you take care of end of life issues such as power of attorney, living wills, prearrangements and many others, go to:

www.freeforms.com and www.uslegalforms.com

Free Estate Planning Kit
Call toll free 1-800-318-5140
Or on the Internet – www.armywill.com